W9-BCZ-990

ROMANCE and REALISM
in
SOUTHERN POLITICS

ROMANCE
and
REALISM
in
SOUTHERN
POLITICS

T. HARRY WILLIAMS

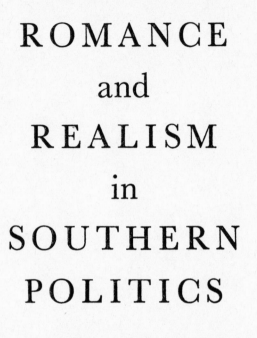

EUGENIA DOROTHY BLOUNT LAMAR

MEMORIAL LECTURES, 1960

Delivered at Mercer University on November 15, 16,
and 17

UNIVERSITY OF GEORGIA PRESS

ATHENS

To
MISS EDITH
Last of the Romantics

Contents

Foreword

THOREAU ONCE WROTE THAT POLITICS IS "THE GIZZARD OF society, full of grit and gravel, and the two political parties are its opposite halves, which grind on each other." The Sage of Walden Pond gave politics the function of simplifying the issues so that the truth might be separated from the chaff and made more digestible to the people. In the South, one of the few areas where both gizzards and politics are enjoyed with great zest, no such function of simplification is evident. Southern politics is a morass of paradoxes, ambiguities, and incredible situations.

Those outside the South need only a limited vocabulary to describe Dixie politics; such words as *Solid South, carpetbagger, white primary, poll tax, literacy test, filibuster,* and *Southern demagogue* seem to cover the situation neatly. Students of the South, however, find many complexities beneath the surface. For example, the area, although tending to eschew idealism for the "practical" in politics, has produced the greatest liberal idealist in American political life—Thomas Jefferson. Although the South seems to lag behind in social action, the greatest political radical among the Presidents was a Southerner, Andrew Jackson. Although the South is said to be conservative in economic matters, it has sent to the Senate such liberals as Estes Kefauver, Lister Hill, Claude Pepper, and

Frank Graham. And although the South is generally considered to be provincial, internationally minded Southern congressmen supported Wilson, a native Southerner, in his fight for the League of Nations.

No one is better qualified than T. Harry Williams to disentangle the web of Southern politics. The distinguished Boyd Professor of History at Louisiana State University is an authority on the Civil War and an objective student of the South. Familiar with both the old and the new, he is now engaged in completing a study of the Longs of Louisiana. The faculty and students of Mercer University heard his provocative lectures on "Romance and Realism in Southern Politics" with great pleasure; the Lamar Committee hopes that the readers of this volume will receive a measure of the same enjoyment.

With the publication of this fourth series of Eugenia Dorothy Blount Lamar Memorial Lectures, delivered at Mercer University in November, 1960, the Lamar Committee and the University reaffirm their gratitude to the late Mrs. Lamar's wisdom and generosity in endowing this perpetual series of lectures. Mrs. Lamar, a cultural leader in Macon and the South for nearly three-quarters of a century, was keenly interested in the continuation of traditional Southern values amid the kaleidoscope of social and economic changes taking place in the modern South. She left a legacy to Mercer University with the request that it be used to "provide lectures of the very highest type of scholarship which will aid in the permanent preservation of the values of Southern culture, history, and literature."

BENJAMIN W. GRIFFITH, JR., *Chairman*
The Lamar Lecture Committee

Mercer University
Macon, Georgia

Preface

SOMEBODY HAS SAID THERE SHOULD BE SOME RULE IN THE profession that requires historians, at certain stages in their careers, to deliver popular yet scholarly lectures. Such a canon would compel the researcher to halt his constant hunt for new materials and to look back at the information he has already acquired—to think about its meaning and to think how he may present this meaning to the intelligent hearer or reader whose knowledge of history is not that of the specialist. The rule will never be made and, of course, should not be made. But something akin to it exists in the various lectureships supported by some of our universities and colleges. These offer the scholar the incentive to put his thoughts and findings together in the briefest and broadest medium.

Mercer University presented me with such an opportunity by inviting me to deliver the Lamar Lectures in Southern History in November, 1960. The writing or arranging of a set of lectures is, I suppose, a unique experience for any scholar. He will alternately be satisfied and dissatisfied with what he has put down. At one time he will like it very much, thinking that this is the way to say something that needs saying. At another he will be very critical of his efforts, wishing that he knew more about the subject and wondering whether his generalizations are justified. In the end, although he will still see shortcomings and omissions, he will be glad that he has done it. At least, these were my reactions. I am fully aware that in traversing such a large period of Southern history I have ventured into some areas where I cannot speak with the authority of one who has done original research. Still I believe that these essays do contain some fresh facts, and I hope that they will add something to our understanding of that always fascinating enigma: what is the South?

It is also a unique experience to be a guest of Mercer University. The academic and social atmosphere of the school and the city is, indeed, rare. Professors Ben W. Griffith, Spencer King, Jr., and other members of the Lamar Lecture Committee, the faculty and the students and the townspeople all combined their gracious energies to make the visit of Mrs. Williams and myself a memory to be cherished.

T. HARRY WILLIAMS

Louisiana State University
Baton Rouge, La.

LECTURE

ONE

The Distinctive South

WE ARE ACCUSTOMED TO SAYING THAT THERE IS A PLACE called the South and that it is inhabited by an identifiable people known as Southerners. We know that this is so, but many of those who most often tell us about it, including natives of the section, would have trouble defining their phrases if pressed for a formula. Even the specialists, the scholars who study the structure of Southern society—historians, sociologists, political scientists—have had trouble in deciding what made the South distinctive or what elements determined the pattern of Southernism. Ironically enough, in attempting to ascribe reasons for coherence, they have come up with diverse analyses. They have pointed to the South's agrarian economy and its staple crops, its rural society and English gentry ideals, its plantation system and institution of slavery, its conservative way of thought and stable way of life, and its consciousness of race and fixation on race relations. And these are not all the formulas advanced to explain the South. The literary artists, sometimes more perceptive in social analysis than the social scientists, have

1

had their go at the problem. As we might perhaps expect, they have seen the land itself as a powerful factor.
The physical environment was such that it sustained life
without too much expenditure of energy. Not having to
conquer his environment, the Southerner was free to ex-
ploit its pleasures. "Soil, scenery, all the color and anima-
tion of the external world tempted a convivial race to
an endless festival of the seasons," wrote Ellen Glasgow.
"In the midst of a changing world all immaterial aspects
were condensed for the Southern planter into an incom-
parable heartiness and relish for life. What distinguished
the Southerner . . . from his severer neighbors to the
north was his ineradicable belief that pleasure is worth
more than toil, that it is even worth more than profit."

The most recent attempts by historians to explain what
is distinctive about the South have got away from the
older formulas of race, economics, or ruralism. Now the
purpose is to show in what ways the South has not shared
in or has stood apart from the common American tradition. Thus Professor Vann Woodward, who has done so
much to illumine our understanding of the region, points
out that the South has not participated in three of the
great national legends and that its experience in these
areas is quite un-American. In a land of plenty the
South was from the Civil War and until recent times a
region of poverty. In a nation whose history has been
an unbroken success story the South has known "frustration, failure, and defeat." Their heritage affords Southerners no basis for the American conviction that there is
nothing beyond the power of humans to accomplish. In
a society bemused with innocence and optimism the South
has lived with evils—slavery and the aftermath of emanci-
pation—and it does not believe that every evil has an
easy cure. "In that most optimistic of centuries in the
most optimistic part of the world, the South remained

basically pessimistic in its social outlook and its moral philosophy," Woodward concludes. "The experience of evil and the experience of tragedy are parts of the Southern heritage that are as difficult to reconcile with the American legend of innocence and social felicity as the experience of poverty and defeat are to reconcile with the legends of abundance and success."

Professor Woodward is also responsible for another current notion—that more than any other Americans Southerners have a sense of history. This is not to be taken in a literal sense as meaning that the people below the Potomac have an unusual devotion to a full and objective record of their past or that, happily, they read a large number of history books or honor history professors above other savants. Rather, it is, to borrow a phrase that Woodward borrowed from Toynbee, that Southerners know history has happened. They know this because Southern history has been compounded of tragedy and many of the elements of that tragedy are still apparent today. More poignantly than other Americans, they realize that the past impinges on the present, and more often than their fellows in other sections they relate the present to something in the past. Indeed, one commentator, Henry Savage, has suggested that this sense of history is the thing that has made the South an entity. "With the exception of what their history did to them, Southerners are much like Americans anywhere in the country," Savage writes. He adds that outsiders would understand the South better if they realized that Southern differences are solely the products of history.

Although most observers admit the existence of this attachment to the past, not all view it with affection or even amusement. Some have found it irritating and have easily proceeded to the conclusion that it is dangerous. Thus Marshall Fishwick explodes: "How can people who know and intuit so much not know that a constant posture of looking backward is the hallmark of stagnation? Very few of us who purport to be historians know much about history. But everything we do know indicates that history is incapable of running backward."

It may be that the critics on both sides are exaggerating the Southerner's consciousness of history. All of this alleged identification with the past may be only another demonstration of his undoubted great ability to deceive himself as well as to spoof the outsider. And this may be the quality that makes him unique among Americans. Far beyond any native competitors, he is marvelously adept at creating mind-pictures of his world or of the larger world around him—images that he wants to believe, that are real to him, and that he will insist others accept. This is another way of saying that the Southerner is likely to be a romantic and that in many situations he almost certainly will refuse to recognize reality. It is an attitude that has fascinated and frustrated beholders. Harry Ashmore, who admits to both reactions, speaks of the Southerner's "remarkable capacity for unreality, which still enables him to hold out against the logic of arguments and of events." W. J. Cash, in *The Mind of the South,* that brilliant book which has been so praised and so damned but which is always quoted by critics from both sides, dealt caustically with the Southerner's capacity for self-deception: "To say that he is simple is to say in effect that he necessarily lacks the complexity of mind, the knowledge, and above all, the habit of skepticism essential to any generally realistic attitude. It is to say that he is inevitably driven back upon imagination, that his world-construction is bound to be mainly a product of fantasy, and that his credulity is limited only by his capacity for conjuring up the unbelievable."

If we admit here at the beginning that the Southerner

is, more than other Americans, a romantic, it is pertinent
to ask at this point of departure: What are the factors or
forces that have made him what he is? The question is by
nature a slippery one, and the answers perforce must be
elusive. Nor will the vast apparatus of scholarship be of
much help to us. The historian with all his documents
and the social scientist with all his data cannot throw
appreciable light on this problem. But we may with some,
but not complete, confidence turn for possible clues to the
literary artists who have depicted the Southern scene.
There fortunate folk have not been inhibited by the scholar's proper caution in dealing with the inner nature of
man. On the contrary, as is proper with them, they have
felt impelled to explain man in terms of their art. It
would seem significant that in interpreting man, or any
other manifestation of the Southern scene, they give great
weight to the physical environment. Some have believed
that the very nature of the Southern world—the climate,
the colors, the odors, the foliage—militates against reality. That "subtle, murky, slumberous clime . . . swart
hot land of pine and palm . . . the sweet and sensuous
South," wrote James Maurice Thompson. Cash, in one of
his most impressionistic passages, contended that the environment constituted "a sort of cosmic conspiracy against
reality in favor of romance." Describing the land as a
pattern of blurred softness, Cash spoke of the mood it in-
duced: "It is a mood, in sum, in which directed thinking
is all but impossible, a mood in which the mind yields
almost perforce to drift and in which the imagination
holds unchecked sway, a mood in which nothing any more
seems improbable save the puny inadequateness of fact,
nothing incredible save the bareness of truth."

More quotations from the literary community could be
introduced, but if the more mundane-minded suspect the
validity of observations from this source we may summon

a colder witness, a New England Adams. Henry Adams attested the effect the South first had on him in words that might have come from a Southern poet: "The May sunshine and shadow had something to do with it; the thickness of foliage and the heavy smells had more; the sense of atmosphere, almost new, had perhaps as much again; and the brooding indolence of a warm climate and a negro population hung in the atmosphere heavier than the catalpas. The impression was not simple, but the boy liked it: distinctly it remained on his mind as an attraction, almost obscuring Quincy itself." If the Southern scene could almost obscure the stark reality of Quincy in the mind of an Adams, it must have been powerful indeed. With this, let us be content and assume that something in the Southern background produced a tendency toward romanticism in thought and politics.

Of all the mind-pictures created by the romantic Southerner, the greatest, the most appealing, and the most enduring is the legend of the Old South. The minute investigations of the historians, the political scientists, and even the sociologists have not succeeded in destroying it or even seriously modifying it. Even those Southern writers who have believed that the legend was bad for the South, when they have come to write about it, expended their most eloquent passages, so in a perverse way testifying to its attraction.

Cash seems carried away despite himself in describing the image of the South that was, "shimmering there forever behind the guns of Sumter. . . . Perpetually suspended in the great haze of memory, it hung, as it were, poised, somewhere between earth and sky, colossal, shining, and incomparably lovely. . . ." Depicting the growth of the legend after 1865, Henry Savage, who thinks it has held the South in a bondage of prejudice, nevertheless can write: "But in the past, the sky was yet still bright with a shining glory. **Although** it was but afterglow of the glorious sunset of a magnificent day which was done, it was still something with which Southerners could identify themselves to relieve the terrible gloom of their contemporary lot."

This cherishing of an ideal dream-world in the past was both a reflection of the Southerner's capacity for unreality and a cause of his continuing reluctance to face the realities of the modern world; for obviously the myth of a perfect society was a powerful argument against change, against even considering whether there was any need for change. And here we may observe that if the Southerner were as aware of history as some of the writers suppose, he would have pursued a different course in some of the social conflicts of modern times. Presumably a people that have experienced evil, defeat, and repression would realize the advantage of adjustment and accommodation in political relations, techniques not noticeably present in the recent South.

But the legend of the Old South is only one demonstration of the Southern talent for fantasy. We see it in many areas of Southern life and in almost every segment of Southern history. It is in the writings of intellectuals like Donald Davidson, who could declare that the cause of the South in the 1920's was "the cause of civilized society against the new barbarism of science and technology controlled and directed by the modern power state." It was in the speeches of politicians in the depression-ridden 1930's, speeches that ignored the harsh economic realities while harking back to old glories that had been destroyed by alien persecutors. It first appeared when the South emerged as a section, when Southern leaders chose to stake the destiny of a whole people on one issue to be fought for with one strategy.

Historians differ as to the exact date when the South

became an entity, recognized by itself and other areas as a distinct section. Although some scholars claim that the states below the Potomac realized they had separate interests as early as the Constitutional Convention, most put the time much later. There is pretty general agreement that the phenomenon we know as the South was at least taking shape by the 1830's. Certainly Southerners were then becoming aware, and often bitterly so, that they were in some way different from people in the rest of the country. These years witnessed the beginning of the abolitionist attack on slavery, the nullification crisis, and the first burgeoning of the Northern industrial order. Suddenly the Southern states were thrown on the defensive—morally, politically, economically. And it was at this moment, exclaims Henry Savage, that the South was born, "the old South of book and song, romance and tragedy, of adulation and castigation." Essentially the same conclusion was reached by the most thoughtful historian of the region in the 1830's, Charles S. Sydnor. By the close of the decade, Sydnor decided, Southerners had come to have a feeling of "oppression, of defeat, and even of desperation." "From this time onward," he wrote, "it is not always possible to explain Southern actions and attitudes by a rational analysis of the facts in each new episode." To Sydnor the salient development was that for the first time Southerners realized they were different. Although they had possessed a distinctive social system, they had not known it until outsiders told them so. Now and rather abruptly "the Southern mind was turned inward to a consideration of its own society."

Unquestionably the South was under attack in the 1830's. But a people whose institutions are being criticized may react in a number of ways. They may, if they are sure of themselves and their security, disdain the criticisms. They may concoct defenses of various kinds, political and polemical, and of varying intensity. Or they may, if they are adept at accommodating themselves to power, which no Americans are, prepare to accept adjustments in their system that will involve a minimum of dislocation. But the Southern response was none of these. Instead, Southerners assumed the position that their society, lying under the disapproval of not just the North but of the whole Western world, was the highest example of civilization to be found on the planet. Other peoples have looked forward or backward to a golden age, but those of the antebellum South proclaimed that they lived in one. "Surely, Southerners had come a long way from Jefferson and a long way out of reality," Sydnor concluded with apparent sadness. "Fighting to defend their way of life, they had taken refuge in a dream world, and they insisted that others accept their castle in the sky as an accurate description of conditions in the South."

Whatever the precise movement when the South passed from a geographic region to a political section, it is evident that the transition was an ominous one, both for the South and the nation. We cannot say with certainty that the change was inevitable. Given all the factors in the situation—the nature of Northern and Southern opinion, the convulsing currents working in the political system, the transforming upheavals occurring in the economic sphere—it probably was. But one of these factors was particularly important in driving the South into a mood of insecurity and isolation. Then, as in later crises, external attacks would have the effect of solidifying internal divisions in a region that naturally was one of great contrasts. And then, as later, the North would show little understanding of or sympathy for the problems of the South.

Many of the condemnations flung against the South went far beyond the bounds of legitimate social criticism, and were, whether or not mischievously conceived, calculated to inflame Southerners to extreme reaction rather than to calm examination of their society. Witness these examples. From the New York *Tribune:* "The Southern plantations are little less than Negro harems. . . . Of all the Southern presidents hardly one has failed to leave his mulatto children. . . . The South is a perfect puddle of amalgamation." From the New York *Times:* "The Southern character is infinitely boastful, vainglorious, full of dash, without endurance, treacherous, cunning, timid, and revengeful." From a Northern minister: "A foaming fountain of insecurity and alarm, of violence and crime and blood, the institution of slavery is." From *Harper's Weekly:* "Their civilization is a mermaid—lovely and languid above, but ending in bestial deformity."

Under almost constant assault after the 1830's, in its response the South committed almost every political error in the book. First, it permitted the opposition to define the issue, slavery, thus putting itself at an immediate disadvantage. Second, it identified every other issue and, indeed, its whole way of life with the defense of slavery. Finally, as Woodward writes: "Because it identified the internal security of the whole society with the security of its labor system, it refused to permit criticism of that system. To guarantee conformity of thought it abandoned its tradition of tolerance and resorted to the repression of dissent within its borders and the forcible exclusion of criticism from outside."

There had been a time when some of the most intelligent social criticism in vogue emanated from Southerners. Indeed, the South had furnished the most informed critics of the institution of slavery itself. But by 1850 this atmosphere of free inquiry and free expression was gone. No longer could Southerners, as in the days of Jefferson and Mason, disapprove of aspects of life in their sections or agree with the strictures of outsiders and remain hon-

ored at home. Now most Southerners refused even to
view slavery as a discussable question or to consider its
relation to their or man's future. A taboo on the subject,
unofficial but the more stringent and repressive because
it represented the feeling of the community, a kind of folk-
enforcement, enveloped all of Dixie. The taboo extended
to subjects related to slavery even indirectly—to, in fact,
anything that could be considered un-Southern. Nor was
it enough for men merely to observe the taboo, to remain
silent. They must, if they were not to be suspect, speak
out in glorification of slavery, and align themselves active-
ly with its defenders. If this was not enforced conformity
of thought, it was close to it. Certainly that freedom of the
spirit that Jefferson had said was necessary to the good
society did not exist in the South before the Civil War.
There is a grim irony in the situation. Inevitably one
wonders what would have happened to the Sage of Monticello if he had returned to his native section in the 1850's.

It may be objected that in this presentation of the
South there is an apparent glaring paradox. Strait-jacket
conformity does not seem to fit in with the tradition of
Southern individualism. And we know that Southerners,
particularly those of the ruling class, were as individualis-
tic a set of men as America has produced. Mrs. Chesnut
has left us an unforgettable picture of a representative
of the aristocratic order, her father-in-law: "Partly pa-
triarch, partly *grand seigneur,* this old man is a species
that we will see no more; the last of the lordly planters
who ruled this Southern World. His manners are un-
equalled still, but underneath this smooth exterior lies
the grip of a tyrant, whose will has never been crossed.
. . . If a lady's name is given, he uncovers and stands hat
in hand until she passes. He has still the Old World art
of bowing low and gracefully. He came of a race that
would brook no interference with their own sweet will by

man, woman, or devil; but then such manners would clear any man's character, if it needed it." Mrs. Chesnut, ordinarily so perceptive in her judgment, was in this case perhaps misled by mere exterior attractiveness. She was writing at the end of the Civil War when the whole Southern world was about to crash after military defeat, a defeat that in part had been brought about by the very traits in the Southern character that she depicted in her father-in-law. Too many Southerners, and often those in high places, had simply refused to impose on themselves the discipline that modern war demands.

And here we have the resolution of the paradox. Southern individualism was of a particular type. It expressed itself in matters of speech and conduct, in self-assertion, sometimes for its own sake, and in self-will, sometimes just to prove somebody had a will. It could not express itself in other areas because dissent in thought was not generally permitted. Could it be that the conformity of the slave system bred an individualism that helped to destroy the Confederacy? If this be true, we have another irony to add to a long list in Southern history.

Perhaps the greatest error committed by the South in the political battles of the antebellum years was in alienating its natural ally, the West. On a number of issues, primarily economic in nature, the two sections had worked together, often to the South's advantage. There was a strong probability that the alliance might have continued. It did not, and largely because again the South insisted on identifying everything with the one issue of slavery. The South demanded that the West accept its position on the status of slavery in the territories. Now people in the West might have varying feelings about the morality of slavery, some being much agitated on the question and others very little, but they were united on one conviction: they did not want to meet the competition of slave labor in the national domain. And so the South lost the West to the Northeast—by insisting on the acceptance of a system utterly unadapted to the needs of the West.

If this seems like unrealistic strategy, we may point to other examples. To the student of politics it is a matter of marvel that Southerners would let their stand on many issues be determined not by political requirements or realities but by the stand of "the enemy," the Northern antislavery elements. Thus at the time of the debate on the Kansas-Nebraska Bill it was freely admitted all over the South that the measure would be of no practical value to the section and might even injure it. Yet Southerners supported it. The Charleston *Mercury* explained why: "Can the South stand listlessly by and see the bill repealed, when this is made the direst issue against her . . .? There is no alternative for the South. When the North presents a sectional issue, and tenders battle upon it, she must meet it, or abide all the consequences of a victory easily won, by a remorseless and eager foe."

The final and tragic climax to the one-issue strategy came at the Democratic national convention at Charleston in 1860, when Southerners demanded that the party adopt a platform on slavery in the territories that they admitted would bring defeat in November. The Western Democrats refused, the party split into two wings, Lincoln won the election, and the South was left standing alone.

When the Southerners could not get what they wanted at Charleston, they walked out. They departed, says Avery Craven, "under the impression that they were upholding a principle," but in reality most of them did not know what to do and only followed an aggressive few who pretended to know the answer. Hitherto in this review of developments since the 1830's we have stressed that the South had a certain latitude of choice as to the

course it would take and that because of certain factors
in the Southern situation and psychology it took the
wrong course, wrong in the sense that the strategy decided
on defeated its purpose. We can believe this to be true,
and at the same time agree with Craven that in the suc-
cessive crises before 1860, or in the one of that year,
most Southerners simply acted out of a feeling of appre-
hension or frustration. That is, although they may have
had the possibility of choice they were also, to an extent,
controlled by circumstance.

Humans do not always have the freedom of decision
that later scholars may think. There is an element of inevitability in many episodes of history, and the one present in antebellum America may have been particularly
puissant. Much of what happened was not planned or
plotted by anybody. Great changes occurred, but they
were the result of impersonal rather than personal forces.
The North moved ahead into the modern world, while
the South remained static, its economy and society not
greatly different from the colonial period. The South fell
to the status of a minority and blamed the North or, more
accurately, men in the North for its reduction. But no
men had done it, Craven points out. "The Industrial Revolution was the real culprit."

What the Industrial Revolution did was epitomized in
the career of the ablest man to come out of the South since
Jefferson. Nobody has described the tragedy of John C.
Calhoun more eloquently than Craven. By circumstance
and choice, Craven emphasizes, Calhoun was forced into
a position "from which he had to defend slavery when
all the rest of the Christian world was leaving it behind;
he had to defend the political rights of the locality when
all the forces of modern technology and business were
producing interdependence and the need for centralized
efficiency; he had to uphold strict construction of the Con-

stitution when the forward sweep of the whole modern social-economic order demanded a broader view; he had to speak for an agricultural interest and way of life just as industry and the city were about to take over; he was forced to be a voice out of the past while he yet lived. . . ."

Whether it was choice or circumstance or both that impelled the South along the course to secession and the Civil War, we cannot with certainty say. We do know that the course was taken and we know what the results were for the South. The war did many things to the section. Among other things, it ensured that the South would remain a section for a long time to come. History provides a number of examples of civil conflicts between classes or factions diffused throughout a country but few in which the contestants faced each other over some kind of geographical line. In the Civil War it was not just a people that had been defeated but also a distinct region. Even if the South had wanted to forget that it was a section, the North hardly would have permitted it to do so. The South, of course, did not want to forget. Rather, it wanted to remember, perhaps had to remember. "Defeated on the actual ramparts of Virginia," wrote Clarence E. Cason, "the Southerners retired to the ramparts of the mind. Here the glories of the old South became an impregnable castle over which was flown the invincible banner of 'the Lost Cause.' Since reality was unbearable, mythology became supreme." It was now that the legends of the Old South of the golden age before Sumter and of the Lost Cause destroyed in the guns after Sumter came to fullest fruition. Perhaps the legend-making was necessary in the conditions prevailing immediately after Appomattox. We are accustomed to saying that the war set the South back economically, but we forget that it also did something perhaps more serious—it threw the South back culturally and socially a century. This being so, Southerners could hardly be expected to respond to all situations in contemporary terms. But we shall have occasion to note that they would cling to the legends long after the circumstances existing in the postwar years had changed if not disappeared.

We have stressed that in the politics of the Old South there was a theme—others, of course, could be developed—and in treating it we have used words like romance and unreality. That is, we have tried to say that in large part politics did not operate in its normal or proper sense to resolve and compromise class and group differences while at the same time maintaining that plurality of opinion ordinarily found in democratic societies. There was a singular oneness about Southern politics—by the 1850's, for all practical purposes, only one party existed; the defense of the section against outside attack was identified with one issue; and the defense was pitched to one strategy.

It has been argued that all of this indicates a tendency to lose reality, to live in a Never-Never land. But after 1865 the South would emerge into a new world. Many of the forces that had molded it had gone with the war. Would the politics of this new South be different from that of the old? Would Southerners learn something from the tragic past that would change their future? In the lectures to come we propose to examine three episodes in the history of the newer South, to see what some Southerners tried to do to meet problems that were both old and new, and to note what was the fate of those efforts.

LECTURE

TWO

The Politics of Reconstruction

WITHOUT A DOUBT THE RECONSTRUCTION ERA IS THE LEAST understood period in our history. This is true for a variety of reasons, and one of the most important of these is that the historical writing about it does not conduce to understanding. We know a great deal about what happened, but there is little consensus as to what the events mean. Taken as a whole, the literature is marked by sentiment and sectionalism, by pride and prejudice, by anger and anguish. No other subject, with the possible exception of the causes of the Civil War, has excited so much controversy and disagreement among scholars. In writing about Reconstruction, historians have been influenced, far beyond their wont in other fields, by prevailing trends in the culture of their own time. Back in the 1920's and 1930's, when the disillusionment following World War I was at its height, Reconstruction was depicted as something pretty horrible—as the stupid aftermath of a stupid resort to war. Andrew Johnson was a hero, and the South was a section crucified on a cross of revenge. Now in our day, when war is viewed as perhaps a necessary instrument to attain right ends and when the racial crusade influences men's thinking about past racial problems, Reconstruction is undergoing a revision. Andrew Johnson has become a petty politician, and the South got, if not what it deserved, what it might have expected after a lost war. Perhaps eventually out of all this controverting and countercontroverting we will get the synthesis that we so badly need.

Here we will not delve into the broad meaning and motivation of Reconstruction, as tempting as the problem is, but confine ourselves to the South and to the reactions of Southerners to the strange new world they found themselves in after 1865, a subject that in itself is as much misunderstood as anything in Reconstruction. Those observers of the Southern scene who have attempted to describe the popular mind are in general agreement that the effect of Reconstruction was to intensify certain trends or traits already apparent before 1860. Thus in the postwar years Southerners, still creating images of perfection, added the legend of the Confederacy to that of the Old South. Conformity of thought became even more rigid and was even more strictly enforced. Determined not to change in any essential part of its being, the South suppressed new ideas from the outside and still more sternly repressed criticisms from its own people. Before the war, laments Hodding Carter, a man could be something of a nonconformist and survive. "But Reconstruction put an end to Southern tolerance of the homegrown dissenter and critic. From the consequent strait-jacketing the South suffered its most grievous and enduring trauma." The tendency to divorce politics from reality, to view it as something essentially romantic, became more pronounced. Threatened with outside interference before the war, Southerners had begun to act together, and now that the interference had actually come they achieved a folk unity almost unique in the modern world. The result was to narrow political choice to the personal. "Was this candidate or that one more showy and satisfying?" asks W. J. Cash. "Did Jack or Jock offer the more thrilling representation of the South in action against the Yankee and the black man? Here, and here almost alone, would there be a field for choice."

These generalizations are doubtless true in the round, but after reading the contemporary documents, one wonders about some things—if it all was as pat as it sounds, if everything was as fated as it seems to be. One wonders too why some of the material in the documents—material that gives a different picture of Southern reactions—has never got into the books. The explanation would seem to be that most writers who have written about Reconstruction were under the spell of a stereotype and when they saw something contrary to the stereotype they simply could not believe it and hence did not use it. For instance, we know now, but have only recently learned it, that in Reconstruction there was relatively little legal segregation of the races, of the system that eventually would be known as Jim Crow. Legal segregation, incidentally, would not come until later, roughly around the turn of the century; and when it was proposed to establish, for example, segregation on streetcars some newspapers objected on the ground there was no need for a change in existing practices. Ironically, fifty years later when the issue was desegregation of public transportation, the identical newspapers objected and again on the ground that the present situation was satisfactory, all of which suggests the intriguing possibility that Southerners are not for segregation or against integration but only against change.

In the earlier writings about Reconstruction there is almost no mention of Southern attitudes on segregation.

The apparent assumption was that all Southerners were for it and that it existed. Beyond a doubt practically all Southerners believed that the Negroes in their midst were in some way inferior and that in a general fashion they should occupy a subordinate position. But almost any examination of the documents will reveal that on the broad subject of race relations Southerners had all kinds of diverse opinions, opinions that would seem as unbelievable to later generations as they must have to the historians who ignored them. Consider these statements from Louisiana sources. In 1873, when a movement to bring about political co-operation between the races was being discussed, the objection arose that political association might lead to social or even sexual equality. Whereupon a New Orleans woman wrote a letter to the press and met the question with startling frankness. "As for miscegenation," she said, "we had it before the war. But, let me ask, was it white women who bore colored children, or the reverse? . . . A negro mother can compel something now; before she was powerless."

Former Governor Paul O. Hébert proclaimed his views just as openly. "Why," he asked, "should not a well behaved, respectable, decently dressed colored man have a box at the theatre, and a stateroom on a steamboat, board and lodging at a hotel, a drink at a public barroom, a sleeping berth on a railroad—if he is able and willing to pay for the same in the legal currency of the country?" He had eaten in restaurants in France where Negroes were present, Hébert went on, and had become accustomed to it. "Travel cures many prejudices—so should a disastrous war." Even if the Negro were given all the privileges enjoyed by the white man nothing much would come of it, Hébert said. "It's his business, like others, to establish his social status—as he makes his social bed he must sleep on it. We must not 'taboo' him or place any obstructions in his way." Another former governor, Alexandre Mouton, offered the same counsel. Grant the Negro all the rights of citizenship, he said, and forget about social questions: "As to this matter of social equality, it is but a scarecrow. No law can regulate, much less control it; it must be left to seek its own level. Every man is responsible for *his* associations, but his neighbor will always do as he pleases and judge for himself."

A country paper, the Thibodaux *Sentinel,* not willing to go as far as some of the people in New Orleans, nevertheless conceded that Negroes were subjected to some gross discriminations: "That an injustice is done to the colored race on steamboats and railroads we have always contended. The steamboats do not allow the colored passengers to occupy a seat in the Cabin, make them wait for their meals until all the white passengers have been supplied, and do not allow them to occupy a state room. . . . When the colored man pays five dollars for a fare on a steamboat he is entitled, and should be given the same accommodations as a white man who pays an equal amount—and if steamboat owners will make a distinction of races they should make a like distinction of prices." And so should the railroad owners, the paper added, and at the same time make white men stop spitting on the floors of cars.

More statements in similar vein could be introduced, but these examples should suffice to show that some men in the South reacted to the racial situation created by the war in a way not usually thought of as typically Southern and certainly in a manner not often depicted in the books about Reconstruction. These men were, almost entirely, from the upper income groups, the planter and business classes. More pragmatic than traditional, they were willing to subordinate the race question to others that they considered more important. If they had succeeded, they would have inaugurated a bold new departure in Southern politics. They did not succeed, and probably their failure proves that they could not have carried their program. But if we believe that not everything in history is fated to happen as it did, we must assume that they might have brought it off, even if in only one or two states. At the least, their efforts demonstrate that Southern thinking about Reconstruction was more fluid than has been supposed and that the South was offered more than one choice as to the course it would follow.

One of these choices is described in this essay. It was presented to Louisiana, and the men behind it were Louisianians, businessmen and planters, who believed they were proposing something that would benefit their class and their state. It was a movement in one state, then, but it has connotations for the story of the whole South in Reconstruction. Although each Southern state differed from every other one in some way, all of them were broadly similar in psychology and purpose. There is evidence that movements like the one in Louisiana occurred in some other states, although perhaps not on as formidable a level.

When the victors in the war proposed to grant the suffrage to the Negroes in the defeated section, Southern whites of every class rallied against the idea. The white masses—farmers, middle class whites, poor whites, all those who because of their economic status may be classified as common whites—were violently opposed to Negroes having the right to vote or, for that matter, of achieving any privilege that suggested equality. The evidence for this conclusion, derived from voting returns, travelers' accounts, and other sources, is strong, although unfortunately we cannot adequately describe the motives that animated these people. Not given to analyzing their feelings or to leaving social records, they have not told us all the things we would like to know. But everything that we do know indicates they were moved by racial concepts. Very simply, they believed that Negroes were inferior, and they were determined to keep the colored race in an inferior position. It was an attitude they would maintain consistently through the whole course of Reconstruction.

The planter-business class, small in numbers but powerful in wealth and prestige, also was opposed to Negro suffrage. And like the common whites, these upper-income whites were influenced by racial notions: they regarded Negroes as inferior. But in their reaction there was an economic as well as a racial element, and, to judge from Louisiana sources, the former outweighed the latter. Put most bluntly, Southern men of property saw the granting of the vote to Negroes as giving power to a propertyless class, and they opposed it because they feared it would lead to an attack on property. In short, they responded as other propertied minorities did in other countries in the nineteenth century to proposals to enfranchise the laboring class, thereby demonstrating that they were, in the spirit of the century, primarily economic beings. The possibility that the national government would install Negro suffrage in the South caused the New Orleans newspapers to examine thoughtfully the whole matter of suffrage and particularly the implications of universal suffrage. Some of the editorials are unusually revealing. The *Times,* an able journal and a spokesman of the business interests, gave the subject the fullest attention. "There was a time when universal suffrage was regarded as one of the grandest features of American institutions," began the *Times,* but it had been demonstrated, especially in large cities, that universal suffrage meant, in effect, the rule of the mob. "The right to vote should be given to those only who can use it with discretion and sound judgment, and as our electoral privileges are already too wide, it would be the maddest folly to extend them at once to a class who have been always under control, and who—without the ability to form a correct judgment for themselves—would be left to the tender mercies of party tricksters."

In a fuller exposition the *Times* said: "Wherever voters greatly outnumber property holders, property assuredly will be unsafe. When voters have property and intelligence, there is some hope that they may 'find their interest in the interest of the community'. . . . Were universal negro suffrage to be added to the white universal suffrage now existing in the South, the security of both life and property would be greatly weakened. . . . With our present too widely extended suffrage it is difficult even now to steer between the rocks of the political Scylla and the whirlpool of its Charybdis, and with universal negro suffrage added, the task would be wholly hopeless." Summarizing its position, the *Times* snapped: "If representative institutions are to prevail in this country, the control of taxes must be left to those who pay them, and the protection of property to those who own it."

Other papers spoke in similar vein. The *Picayune* announced that it opposed Negro suffrage, not because the Negroes were colored, but because the principle of universal suffrage was wrong. "We look upon it [voting] as a duty rather than a right," said the *Picayune*, "and regret that there is so much of it among the whites." Universal suffrage was "the unlimited suffrage of the ignorant, landless and lawless."

The *Crescent*, noting that such leaders as Wade Hampton and Alexander H. Stephens had suggested extending the suffrage to Negroes who had acquired property, said: "Southern conservatives ask nothing more on the

subject of suffrage than that its distribution shall be determined by the test of character and intelligence. They
have asked for nothing more from the time that, by one
of the irreversible results of the war, the Southern negroes became a part of the free population of the country. It is not their fault if such a test has been rejected
in favor of another that proscribes a large proportion of
the highest intelligence on the one hand, and opens all
political functions to the maximum of ignorance on the
other hand." And again the *Crescent* said: "It seems to
be practically absurd to commit the decisions of these
difficult questions to numbers of extemporized citizens incapable of forming any accurate or rational opinions; and likely to imagine that the right to vote means
the right to live without work, and to rob the industrious
classes for the benefit of the idle and thriftless."

The Republicans or the Northern power-groups, or
however we choose to label the coalition of the victors,
disregarded Southern objections to Negro suffrage on
whatever grounds; in 1867 Congress enacted the Reconstruction Acts, and the thing was a reality at last. There
followed the period and the process we commonly think
of as Reconstruction—the Negro became a political power (the extent of his power has been exaggerated), the
scalawag and the carpetbagger had their day, and corruption and violence afflicted the land. It is beyond our scope
here to examine the various facets of Reconstruction, but
one, crucial to an understanding of the process and of
the reactions of upper-class whites, must be noted. Reconstruction was in large part a government of and for if
not by poor men. The colored masses, upon whom the
Republican organizations in the Southern states depended
for votes, demanded a program of social services furnished
by government, something very much like the modern
welfare state, and the Republican bosses necessarily had to

concede some of the aspirations of these most humble but most numerous of their followers. The bosses also had to gratify the desires of other members, not humble and white as well as colored, for graft.

It was all very expensive. State budgets soared to heights that horrified people who remembered the economical prewar days when government provided almost no services. Higher and higher taxes had to be voted, and under the system then prevailing the brunt of the taxes fell on real property. By the votes of poor men the propertied minority, the planter-business class, was being subjected to a killing tax burden. Caught in an economic squeeze, the men of this class would respond to Reconstruction in economic terms and as economic creatures. They would respond by trying to control the Negro vote in their own economic interest, for as narrow an object as lower taxes. But beyond this immediate interest, they attempted something bolder—by making certain concessions to the colored race they hoped to subordinate the race issue in politics and possibly to remove it altogether.

Even before the full pinch of the welfare program was felt, immediately after Negro suffrage became a force in politics, upperclass whites moved to control the Negro vote. Their action was entirely natural, almost like a conditioned reflex. As recent slaveholders, they were accustomed to dealing with Negroes, whom they considered an inferior and childlike race; they now expected that their former chattels would follow their instructions in politics as they had in the fields. Indeed, some leaders of the farmers opposed the advent of Negro suffrage for the very reason that the planters would dominate the colored voters. These men envisioned the lords of the plantations marching Negroes to the polls in droves to carry elections against the common whites. It would never happen that way. The rich whites were not able to manipulate effectively the Negro vote in any election. But they tried to, stubbornly over a period of years and resourcefully with a number of devices.

One device was to attempt to absorb the Negroes into the state and local organizations of the Democratic party. The bait held out was recognition of those political and legal rights of the race already established by national laws and the allocation of some offices to colored candidates. Exactly how far this strategy was carried we do not know. Partial research indicates that there was much more of a Democratic approach to the Negroes than has been suspected. As late as 1870 the platform of the Louisiana Democrats pledged this recognition of Negro rights: "The interests of both white and black men are identical in this struggle. Whatever rights and privileges either enjoy under the constitution are sacred, and it is the duty of every citizen to see that they are maintained." Negroes were welcomed to Democratic rallies, and sometimes Negro orators spoke from the same platform with whites.

As to Negro candidates on Democratic tickets, we know there were a number in several states. The psychology of their white sponsors is revealed in a news story recounting the plan of New Orleans businessmen to put up Negroes as candidates for Congress, mayor, and other places. For Congress the backers had their eyes on a Negro who would "protect and do more for the South than any white Radical which can be selected to run against him. . . . The merchants are taking an unusual interest in being represented in Congress by a representative born in the South. The nearer approach to a real African, black in color the better." The whole ticket, it was assured, would bear comparison with any members of the Republican slate: "It will be composed of faithful and good citizens, formerly in the service of our old residents."

The records do not disclose the eventual outcome of

all the schemes to run Negro Democrats, but it would seem there was more talk than action. The New Orleans project just described, for example, never materialized. Probably, in some cases the white leaders realized that the white masses would not accept too many black candidates. More probably, aspiring Negro politicians with an eye to the future preferred to join the Republicans. In the ranks of the new party, new in the South, Negro leaders could feel more secure and more important. While white Democrats might parade Negroes around in campaigns, they obviously did so because they thought they had to, because they wanted something from the Negroes. There was a large element of condescension in everything they said and did. And although they might speak grandly and generally of the Negroes' rights, they drew the line at anything suggesting personal equality. This attitude on the part of the whites explains why a second device they adopted to control the colored vote failed—the device of joining the Republicans and working from within.

The term scalawag is a familiar one in Reconstruction history. Commonly it is a term of opprobrium—the scalawag is the Southerner who deserted his own people and joined the enemy Republicans. The image of the scalawag is that of an adventurer, an unscrupulous man, a nobody after power and pickings. Doubtless there were scalawags who were all of these things, but the image is one of the great historical myths. It is hardly realized, even by historians, how much of the fabric of Radical Reconstruction was the work of native Southerners. For example, in the Mississippi constitutional convention there were 17 Negroes, 20 Northerners or, to employ the usual term, carpetbaggers, 19 Democrats, and 29 scalawags. In the South Carolina convention 27 of the approximately 124 delegates were scalawags. For Georgia the figures are almost startling: 37 Negroes, 9 carpetbaggers, 12 Democrats, and probably 111 scalawags. Republicans ruled Alabama for several years after 1868, and the roster of their leaders is revealing. Over one-third of the congressmen were native whites, and the two governors were Southern-born, as were the three supreme court justices. Of 76 prominent Republicans—holders of the big offices —45 were scalawags, 24 were carpetbaggers, and 7 were Negroes.

If the number of scalawags and their large role seems at variance with the stereotype of Reconstruction, their origin or status will probably seem more so. Not many studies of who the scalawags were have been made, but the available evidence indicates that they came from the upper classes or the professional groups allied with those classes. Professor David Donald, who has analyzed the situation in Mississippi, concludes that in that state most of the former Whigs, in antebellum times the party of the big slaveholders, went into the Republican party and stayed there for years. "Such action is not hard to understand," Donald writes. "The Whigs were wealthy men —the large planters and the railroad and industrial promoters—who naturally turned to the party which in the state as in the nation was dominated by business interests." Donald also finds, and his opinion seems to be supported by the story in other states, that the scalawags at first were fairly successful in controlling the Republican organization but that they eventually lost their leadership to the carpetbaggers. They lost because they would not go as far as their rivals in promising social equality and in voting large appropriations for welfare. But it was only after a long and determined effort, Donald emphasizes, that they gave up and drifted "slowly and reluctantly over to the Democratic camp."

The planter-business group had tried to entice the Negroes to join the Democrats and they had failed. They had tried the expedient of themselves joining the Republicans to control the Negroes, and they had failed again. But they still attempted yet another device. This was to invite the Negroes to leave the Republican party and unite with them in a new organization separate from the Democrats. The whites pledged that in return they would recognize the Negroes' civil and political rights. Such movements, varying in the scope of the promises extended by the whites, were launched in several states. The most elaborate one was the Louisiana Unification Movement of 1873. It is surely one of the most significant episodes in Reconstruction history.

The Louisiana movement came at a time when white hopes for the future had hit a new low after the election of 1872, which the Democrats or conservatives claimed to have won only to see the national government recognize the Republican claimants. Tension between the races flared out in savage violence, trade and investment languished, real estate fell in value—but the tax rates remained high. To people in the upper income class it seemed that the very material basis of the state was being destroyed, while they themselves were subjected to a confiscatory tax burden. The situation that produced the movement, then, was compounded of political and racial elements, but the strongest one was economic in nature. The men who would sponsor the movement were almost without exception conscious of race and racial differences, but under the strain of economic distress they acted to remove race as an issue in politics.

In the spring of 1873 rumors were heard in New Orleans that a number of prominent whites and prominent Negroes—it turned out there were fifty from each group— were at work on a plan to unify the races into one great organization that would win control of the state and end

Reconstruction. Immediately approving letters and inter-
views flooded the press. Many of these statements came
from businessmen and voiced a completely economic approach to politics and the race problem. Thus a merchant
described as "one of our oldest and best" said: "Approve
of it! It is our only hope of salvation. The negroes, unless
drawn over to us, will constantly elect carpet-baggers.
Their election means increased taxation, and this means
total and absolute ruin. Our people cannot be so blind
as not to see and comprehend this." A real estate owner
exclaimed: "On with unification for God's sake, if it will
give us an honest government; our present lot is insup-
portable." A "prominent" merchant declared: "I am in
favor, in case we ever have another election, of giving
to the colored people the bulk of the lucrative positions.
. . . I am not afraid that they will, in any considerable
degree, abuse their privileges, and, for ourselves, we
want nothing but peaceful government."

An anonymous writer advised granting the Negroes the
representation their numbers entitled them to: "We
cannot afford to let the opportunity slip. Unless the two
races adopt some platform on which they can stand on
friendly terms, Louisiana has nothing to look forward to
but debt, dissension, anarchy." A "conservative" leader
agreed that a new party must be organized: "There are
many foolish prejudices and fears on both sides that
must be eradicated. . . . We must . . . satisfy the reasonable
demands of the negroes. This accomplished, Louisiana
will again blossom as the rose. It is our only salvation."

Running through most of the statements was the theme
that the race issue was a false one in politics and that
by harping on it the politicians had driven the Negroes
into the hands of the Republicans. One "Progress" declared: "There stands between us and the truth a horde
of noisy demagogues, who mislead us as completely as

the wily carpet-bagger hoodwinks the credulous negro.
And here is our great error." "Juvenus" warned the whites
that the situation demanded that they rise "superior to
past traditions, party lines, and dead or useless issues."
Especially blunt on this matter was "Sigma," who said:
"We have, I believe and hope, reached that point in the
history of a proud people in adversity, where, broken by
accumulated disaster and destroyed by our own passions,
we are at length willing to recognize that the future must
renounce the prejudices of the past. . . ."

Reading all these expressions, a columnist for one of the
papers was moved to say: "But an era has arrived when,
having been chastened by afflictions not wholly unde-
served, it would seem that the mass of men are fast re-
ceding from old landmarks of intolerance and prejudice;
when they are casting about them for better guidance
than that beneath whose auspices they have been well
nigh stranded."

Practically every newspaper in the city came out in support of the general principle of unification. The only dis-
senters were Republican organs, obviously alarmed at what
the new departure might do to their party. Leading the
press chorus of approval was the conservative *Times,*
which had helped to instigate the movement and now became its most vociferous champion. "We are at the dawn
of a new dispensation," predicted the *Times* as it welcomed unification. "Politically, old things are passing
away and all things are becoming new. . . . To this end
there should be a common agreement, embracing all races,
colors and conditions, and if such agreement were con-
scientiously made and faithfully complied with, the redemption of Louisiana would become at once assured."
The *Times* was privy to the identity of the white sponsors
of unification, and it trusted to the distinguished background of these men to overcome objections that the

movement was going too fast: "It may be impracticable at first to totally obliterate prejudices which are the growth of centuries, but if 'our oldest and best' set the example, the way will gradually become easy, and the beauty of harmony will carry with it an approving sanction which cannot long be resisted."

Other journals were not as enthusiastic and optimistic as the *Times,* but they voiced support for a political unification, that is, one not involving social rights. The *Herald,* known as an extreme Democratic paper, called for acceptance of all the constitutional rights presently guaranteed to Negroes: "And such acceptance ought to be based not on a mere party policy, but on the democratic truth and justice of these constitutional demands. . . . We must honestly turn our backs upon the past, commit to an eternal oblivion the stubborn and ancient prejudices which are now at war with the fundamental ideas of our democratic system." The *Picayune,* leading organ of the conservative Democrats, took the same line: the whites must recognize the political rights of the Negroes but no more. "We heartily assent to give the colored race all the political rights and privileges under the law, the white race possesses," declared the *Picayune.* "Let there be an end of prejudice and proscription, and for the future let there be no difference of opinion dividing our people except upon questions of governmental polity."

While the press and the public discussed the broad principles of unification, the white and colored sponsors of it, a Committee of One Hundred, composed, it was said, of "Southern gentlemen" and the "wealthiest and most intelligent colored men," were at work on a specific plan. Finally it was announced that after weeks of deliberation the Committee would meet on June 16 to consider and adopt a platform. On that day the men behind the movement were at last revealed to the state.

Isaac N. Marks, one of the most prominent figures in the business and civic life of New Orleans and before the war a leading Whig, presided. General P. G. T. Beauregard, late a full general of the Confederacy and now a war hero and a railroad promoter, headed the committee on resolutions. The fifty white sponsors were the business and professional leaders of the city, including the presidents of practically every bank and corporation in New Orleans. The colored backers were the wealthy, cultured aristocracy of the race, many of them coming from the so-called "Creole Negroes" who had been free before the war.

Beauregard was generally regarded as the head of the movement, but although he was sharply interested in devices to control the Negro vote and had been for years, it is probable that the real guiding spirit was Marks, who had been working for something like the present plan for over a year. Not too much is known about Marks. He was obviously a man of some culture, and he must have had great courage to say the things he did. His views on the place of the race issue in politics were a blend of pragmatism and principle. In one of his public statements in support of unification he said: "The old Bourbon writers of the defunct Democratic party; the extreme negro-baiting graduates of the ante-bellum State Rights school— those, whose religion it is to believe that the negro can neither be educated nor elevated—a portion of the Carpet-bag element in the Republican party, all unite in denouncing the movement and in declaring it a failure. . . . It cannot fail, unless charity and justice have ceased to exist among our people, and we are determined to continue to blindly battle against *accomplished facts*, as we have done so suicidally since the close of the war."

Did white Louisianians think that the Thirteenth, Fourteenth, and Fifteenth amendments would be repealed, Marks asked. Then let them join with the colored people in this movement that would put the state in a position to treat with the national government. Until something like unification was consummated, Louisiana would never secure a hearing in the North: "We may raise hundreds of thousands of dollars, and we may employ politicians even more crafty and flexible than those who have already tried their hands; until we can prove to Congress and the people of the country that we have ceased to deprive *one half of the voting population* of the State of their just rights as citizens, we will continue to sacrifice our time, our labor, and our money."

Here Marks was employing a straight pragmatic argument: we must recognize the inevitable. But beyond mere immediacy he believed that if the whites, as was their religious duty, educated the Negro, he could be elevated to a position where he could act responsibly. Had not the Negro proved during the war and after that despite powerful pressures to the contrary he had an "innate sense of justice" and a "human soul"? Declaring his belief that the colored race could be uplifted, Marks said: "It is my determination to continue to battle against these abstract, absurd and stupid prejudices, and to bring the whole force of my character, and all of the little talent I possess, to break them down. They must disappear; *they will disappear.*"

It can be surmised that most of the men at the June 16 meeting did not share all of Marks' feelings or even approve them. But they desperately desired a return to economic stability and honest government and lower taxes, and they were willing to go to great lengths to attain their ends. The meeting unanimously adopted the platform recommended by Beauregard's committee. It was a remarkable document, both in the view of race relations it expressed and in the strategy it proposed to subordinate the race issue in politics. Twenty-five or fifty or seventy-five years later Louisianians probably would not believe that General Beauregard had ever put his name to such a statement.

Entitled "An Appeal for the Unification of the People of Louisiana," it recited that the state was threatened with death in every vital organ of its being and could be saved only by a unification of all its people, white and colored, in a new party. To achieve this great end, the whites would have to make a number of concessions to the Negroes, and the platform detailed what these concessions should be. It advocated the "equal and impartial exercise" by every citizen of "every civil and political right" guaranteed by the federal Constitution and laws and by "the laws of honor, brotherhood and fair dealing." Specifically, the platform recommended abandonment of segregation in "places of public resort," namely, establishments operating under public license; on "vehicles of public conveyance," namely, railroads and steamboats; and in the public schools. It advocated that corporations recognize the right of colored stockholders to be represented on boards of directors, that planters consider the possibility of selling parts of their holdings to Negroes, thus fostering a "political conservatism which is the offspring of proprietorship," and that industrial employers make no racial distinctions in hiring workers. Finally, the platform advised that because of the population equality between the races there should be an equal division of state offices, presumably on the ticket of the unification party.

The Unification Movement was now officially launched, and its sponsors announced that on July 15 a mass meeting would be held in New Orleans to register public ratification of the platform. Now Beauregard issued a statement urging the state to accept unification. His argument was completely pragmatic. Already, in the sense of legal recognition, the Negroes had political and civil equality, he pointed out. But the carpetbaggers had the Negroes. Why? Because the whites refused to extend even a symbolic recognition of the Negroes' rights. Let the whites recognize these rights, and the colored people, who were also Southerners, would desert the alien carpetbaggers and flock to the native whites, who alone could ensure that Negro rights would be real and enduring. In short, the races were arrayed against each other on an issue of no great moment.

Beauregard was saying to the whites: Let us eliminate this issue and get on to other things or, as he put it, to "more important aims." He dismissed objections that the Unification platform would bring about governmental interference in private social relations. "These lie entirely outside the domain of legislation and politics. It would not be denied that, in travelling, and at places of public resort, we often share these privileges in common with thieves, prostitutes, gamblers, and others who have worse sins to answer for than the accident of color; but no one ever supposes that we thereby assented to the social equality of these people with ourselves. . . . By the enjoyment in common of such privileges neither whites nor blacks assert, or assent to, social equality, either with each other or even between individuals of the same race."

In New Orleans reactions to the Unification platform and to Beauregard's appeal were generally favorable. Some people and part of the press voiced irritation that the plan went beyond political union; there was particular criticism of the proposal for nondiscrimination in hiring, but the tone of the objections was only that this idea was absurd and could never be practical. Some doubters asked why the whites were making all the concessions.

What would the Negroes give in return? The unifiers replied that the colored leaders were pledged to deliver the votes of their followers to the new party.

But the fate of Unification would not be determined in New Orleans. It was a product of the city and of city businessmen, some of whom, like Beauregard, had plantation ties, but to accomplish its purpose it would have to win acceptance by the whites in the country parishes. In the southern parishes such acceptance seemed to be forthcoming. The Opelousas *Courier* agreed with Beauregard that dead issues should be removed from politics: "We mean by dead issues, such as have passed from the domain of politics to that of law, constitutional and statutory; for instance, such as the civil and political rights of colored citizens."

The Donaldsonville *Chief* stressed that the races were necessary to each other. The whites needed the Negroes to oust the carpetbaggers and the blacks needed the whites to perfect their privileges. All the whites had to do was to recognize the rights the Negroes already had in law. "Is there anything in it? Will we be any better off? Shall we resign our last remaining privilege? Gentlemen, that privilege is hollow to the core, and the experiment, we candidly believe, is worth a trial." Expressions such as these came only from south Louisiana, a plantation area, and reflected the views of upper-class whites, who, like their fellows in New Orleans, wanted above all else to get rid of corrupt government and grinding taxes. Significantly, this was also a region inhabited largely by people of French extraction, who had always had milder racial attitudes than those in the Anglo-Saxon parishes to the north.

It was immediately evident that Unification was not taking in the part of the state roughly north of Baton Rouge. Here the reactions against it were strong, even

violent, and were pitched almost entirely on a racial level.
The Shreveport *Times* denounced the platform as a "monstrosity," and went on to declare: "The battle between
the races for supremacy . . . must be fought out here . . .
boldly and squarely; the issue cannot be satisfactorily adjusted by a repulsive commingling of antagonistic races,
and the promulgation of platforms enunciating as the political tenets of the people of Louisiana the vilest Socialist
doctrines." The Monroe *Ouachita Telegraph* exploded:
"Unification on the basis of perfect equality of whites
and blacks! We abhor it in every fibre of our being. We
know of no necessity that can bring us to such a pass."
Other country papers repudiated the Confederate hero
who headed the Unification Movement: "Shame on you,
Beauregard," and "So we, the people of rural districts,
bid Beauregard a long goodnight." The parish officials of
Catahoula expressed what came to be a motif of the
country reaction—all other questions must be subordinated to racial separation. In words reminiscent of the
pro-slavery defense, these men said: "If the political death
of the State must be the consequence, let us accept it."

Most of the opposition to Unification came from the
small-farmer areas and reflected the intense racial convictions of the common whites. But some of it emanated
from planter areas, such as the Red River valley, where
the upperclass whites were as race conscious as the farmers. It would seem, then, that white attitudes were not
determined completely by economic influences but that
culture and tradition played a part. In New Orleans and
the French southern parishes people were willing to subordinate race to other issues. In the Anglo-Saxon central
and northern parishes people were determined that race
should be the only issue. Whatever the reasons for it, one
thing was plain: the white masses would not accept Unification, they would not pay the price set by Beauregard

to bring the Negroes over to their side. In anguish and anger the unifiers cried that social equality was a false issue and that the actual impact of their program on private relations would be hardly perceptible.

Beset by attacks from their own people, Beauregard and his associates must have noted a great irony—they were subjected to criticism just as un-understanding from the North. Presumably they could have expected support —after all, by Northern standards they were on the side of the angels—or, at least, sympathy for their objectives. Some Northern papers, it is true, approved Unification but in a condescending tone: can anything this enlightened be happening in the South? The prevailing line was that this was a Southern trick and that the North must keep a wary eye on those behind it. It was a refrain that would be heard later.

Although all the signs pointed to failure, the unifiers went ahead with plans to hold their mass meeting on July 15. At this gathering Marks again presided, and he made the opening address. But Beauregard and some of the other sponsors, perhaps sensing what was coming, found reasons to be absent. Of the five speakers, three were Negroes, and if Unification was not dead these colored leaders killed it. Heretofore the Negroes participating in the movement had been businessmen like the whites, and like the whites amateurs in politics. They earnestly desired racial co-operation, but they were never quite sure that they could trust the whites. Like the Northern press, they found it hard to believe that Beauregard and his associates meant what they said. Now the professional Negro politicians took a hand in the matter, and their intervention indicates that Unification still had a chance; at least, that it had some attraction for the colored masses. The politicians had an obvious motive for wanting Unification to fail—if it succeeded they were in danger of losing their place and power in the Republican party. It seems plain that they set out deliberately to torpedo the movement. The Negro speakers said, in so many words: We congratulate you whites on trying to overcome your prejudices, we will help and guide you on the upward way, and if you really repent we will work with you politically. One of the Negro leaders read a pledge designed to answer the criticism that the whites were making all the concessions to achieve Unification. This document recited that when the Negroes received full recognition of their civil and political rights, but not until then, would they join with the whites to return honest government to the state. Curiously, these Negro leaders were acting in the same way as most white leaders—they were insisting that there was only one issue in politics and that this issue should absorb all others. They were doing what Henry C. Warmoth, former Republican governor, had once warned them not to do on the issue of civil rights—attempt an immediate and complete victory.

Everybody knew now that the Unification Movement was finished. The white masses would not accept it, and the colored politicians would not let their people accept it. In north and central Louisiana there was rejoicing that the "vile thing" had been repudiated. But in the southern parishes there was a feeling of regret, even of sadness, that a promising experiment was being dropped; people felt that somehow the state had taken a wrong turn. Writing off Unification as a failure, one country paper said: "The black man of Louisiana is wedded to his idols. The carpet-bagger and the scalawag . . . have a firm, a death-like hold on him. . . ." The *Picayune,* an extreme Democratic journal that had supported Unification with some qualifications, spoke sorrowfully of the refusal of the Negroes to go along with the movement: "They are unwilling to meet the white man on common

ground, with common laws and common privileges, and
struggle with him to achieve the redemption of all from
ruin, and thus overcome the prejudices which divide and
ruin; but they demand that the white man shall come
with bated breath and stoop that they may step forward. The great mass of our people would willingly concede to the colored people the civil and public rights of
citizens, which they claim, if they could see the colored
people sincerely laboring for a reduction of taxation and
for an honest and economical administration." The *Times*
was not convinced that the Negroes alone had killed Unification; rather, everybody had had a hand in the act:
"The traditional impracticability of this community
stepped in and finished it. . . . The trouble was that Gen.
Beauregard & Co., being thoughtful gentlemen, appealed
to a sense of kindness and justice and magnanimity that
was slightly inaccessible."

All of the analysts, those who rejoiced that Unification had failed and those who regretted, ascribed its collapse to one set of men or one factor. And all were right,
but only in part. Many people and diverse forces were
responsible for the death of the movement. The men who
had supported it and the men who had opposed it, the
planters and the politicians, the whites and the blacks,
were actors in one of those episodes that together make
up the drama we call history. They had performed their
parts in different ways and for different reasons. Some had
acted out of deliberate choice in full knowledge of what
they were doing, some, perhaps, under the influence of
forces of which they were unaware, and some because
they could conceive of no other way to act.

The historian can look back at this episode, as at others
in the human record, and see that here was a moment
when possibly the record might have been changed, when
another turn might have been taken. He can speculate,

for example, that Unification might have had a greater
measure of success if its sponsors had avoided social and
economic implications and proposed only a political alliance of the races. Or he can conjecture that even had
it won acceptance, it would not have endured, if for no
other reason than that the planter-business coalition
lacked both the wealth and the will to finance the welfare program the Negroes surely would have demanded.
The historian can wonder about these and other things,
but in the end he must record that Unification failed, as
did other white attempts to subordinate the race problem
and the racial issue, and he must conclude that the great
imperatives, the forces that shape history, had decided
it that way. But he must also record that there was a
surprising plurality in Southern thinking about Reconstruction and that there were Southerners who would have
altered the story if they could.

The New Orleans *Times,* in one of its plaintive obit-
uaries of Unification, asked: "If Unification, meaning
simply peace instead of conflict between the races with
reference to civil and political rights, will not work, then,
in the name of conscience and common sense, what *will*
work?" The answer was not long in coming. It was embodied in the overthrow one by one of the Republican
state governments, sometimes accomplished by normal
political methods and sometimes by methods that were
not so normal. That answer would come to a climax in
1877, and to most people it seemed final. But the question
would be asked again and with a renewed sharpness in
the economic and political convulsions that wrenched the
South in the last two decades of the century. And again,
as in Reconstruction, there would be some Southerners
who proposed answers that might have altered the seem-
ing inevitability of Southern history.

LECTURE

THREE

The Politics of Populism and Progressivism

WILLIAM PERCY, POET AND PLANTER ARISTOCRAT OF THE
Mississippi Delta, could recall that as a boy he had lis-
tened on the gallery of his home to the conversation of the
men who came there to consult with his father—the leaders who ruled the state after the end of Reconstruction.
Percy liked to picture them: "These were the men who,
before I was a listener, bore the brunt of the Delta's
fight against scalawaggery and Negro domination . . .,
who stole the ballot-boxes, which, honestly counted, would
have made every county official a Negro, who helped shape
the Constitution of 1890, which in effect and legally disfranchised the Negro, who still earlier had sent my grand-
father to the legislature to help rid the state of 'old Ames,'
the carpetbag Governor."

There was some exaggeration in Percy's memories. In
no state did the white bosses of the Republican party
allow the Negroes more than a fraction of even the local
offices; during the whole course of Reconstruction in Mississippi there was only one Negro mayor and twelve sheriffs. But his depiction of how the leaders of the New South

44

appeared to themselves and to their class was completely correct. They were leaders because they were destined to lead, "because of their superior intellect, training, character, and opportunity." They knew leadership was a burden, but they also knew that unless they exercised it "government would be bad."

If there seems to be a trace of condescension toward the masses in Percy's analysis of leadership, then consider his description of a crowd addressed by his father in a campaign when the people were beginning to show signs of chafing under planter primacy. In it Percy perhaps revealed more than he realized of the psychology of his class: "I looked over the ill-dressed, surly audience, unintelligent and slinking, and heard him appeal to them for fair treatment of the Negro and explain to them the tariff and the Panama tolls situation. I studied them as they milled about. They were the sort of people that lynch Negroes, that mistake hoodlumism for wit, and cunning for intelligence, that attend revivals and fight and fornicate in the bushes afterwards. They were undiluted Anglo-Saxons. They were the sovereign voters. It was so horrible it seemed unreal."

Not many of the statesmen would have spoken in terms of such utter contempt; they subscribed, even if only ritualistically, to the democratic myth. But apparently it never occurred to them that the sovereign voters might aspire to something more than they were getting—a discussion of economic issues closer to home than the tariff and least of all to an economic life fuller than the one they had. These men who rose to power after 1877 we call the Bourbons or the Redeemers. They and men of their kind who came immediately after them would dominate Southern politics for a long time, until well after the turn of the century, a span comparable to the reign of the chiefs of the Old South. They were the architects who determined the design of the New South. Although they differed from state to state in purpose and philosophy, they show a basic unity. It is possible, to borrow a term from the sociologists, to structure them. They believed in honest government, although in some states the Bourbon administrations rivaled the Reconstruction regimes in corruption. They believed in economical government, the type that furnished few services and collected few taxes. They thought that government should not interfere in social matters or regulate economic affairs. They preached the industrialization of the South through the importation of Yankee capital and the advantages of close co-operation with the industrial East. They were often of the planter class and they acted and talked like traditional Southerners, but they were hardly in the old agrarian tradition. Presumably the men of the Confederacy had not fought to create an industrial society. Or did this mutation of the men of the New South represent the real meaning of the Lost Cause?

On the face of it, the Bourbons did not seem to turn their backs on the past. Indeed, they made deep obeisance before the altar of the Lost Cause and before that other shrine, the Old South. So did all Southerners, and the 1880's saw both traditions assume a fullness and a glory they had never had before. In part, this was only the natural and perhaps necessary nostalgia of a people who had passed through great afflictions. In part, it was but another representation of the Southern propensity to superimpose ideal dream worlds on the world of the present. But it was also, with the political leaders, a deliberately adopted device to attain a particular and practical end. To overthrow Reconstruction the whites had had to achieve a rigid unity of purpose and organization; they had had to submit to unusual restraints of party discipline. The upper-income whites, who had so often followed their own course in race relations, had joined the solid white ranks, and from the revolution that destroyed Republican power they had emerged as the leaders.

Now that the great object was accomplished the wealthy whites—the Bourbons, the Redeemers—were determined to retain their estate by maintaining the disciplines and the devotions of Reconstruction. They would do this by the surest means they knew—by recalling the past, the great past with its radiance and the immediate sad past with its dangers just averted. In the monolithic Democratic party the whites could thresh out their differences; but these differences would never become troublesome because no issue must be permitted to divide white solidarity. It was an admirable arrangement to head off any economic stirrings on the part of the masses. Indeed, it was understood that there was supposed to be no relation between politics and economics. "The fact is that the present Democratic party in Virginia was formed . . . without any reference to economic questions," said one leader in the state of Jefferson. Echoed a Mississippi editor: "In other States it may be different. In this State for some time to come there is but one issue. All know what it is." From statements like these, Professor Vann Woodward was led to conclude that the politics of Redemption was of the romantic type, emphasizing tradition and demanding the subjection of all other issues to one while ignoring the future and denying issues of economics and self-interest.

In one sense this analysis is right but in another it is wrong. During Reconstruction the rich whites had attempted to subordinate racial problems to economic concepts—of a narrow nature, it is true, but nevertheless economic in nature. Failing, they resorted after 1877 to a new strategy, one with a reverse twist but designed to accomplish the same objective. Now they elevated the race issue to subordinate economic or other issues that endangered their position. There was a lot that was old in the politics of the New South, but there was something that was new.

Actually, the Bourbons were never able to fit all the pieces completely into their neat pattern of control. From time to time dissident farmer movements rose to challenge the power structure, boiling up in the Democratic party or spilling over into new organizations usually bearing the name Independent. In addition, there was a vestigial Republican party in almost every state that had to be constantly watched. Contrary to popular impression the Republicans did not disappear with the end of Reconstruction. Between 1877 and 1900 the Republicans polled in national elections in the Southern states a popular vote that varied from forty down to twenty per cent. They could be a definite threat in local elections, particularly if they fused forces with maverick Democrats. None of the various insurrections achieved any real success. The Bourbons were able to face them down by appealing to the loyalties of the past or by stigmatizing the rebels as men who would destroy the bases of white solidarity. When these techniques did not work, the leaders resorted to the ultimate weapon—they used the vote of the Negro to maintain their power. In the name of white supremacy they employed the black man against other white men.

Here it is necessary to recapitulate the psychology of upperclass whites on race relations, as it had developed during Reconstruction and as it would be refined after 1877. These men, it will be recalled, had been willing to make great concessions to the Negro if they could control his vote. They believed in racial differences and some form of racial separation, although in a rather vague way, but they placed economics and power above questions of race. Now in the years after Reconstruction they manifested the same attitudes—on the Negro and on his place in white society and his role in politics. They made no move to establish legal segregation of the races, although they condoned a large measure of unofficial segregation. In their view the Negro was inferior and hence should occupy a subordinate status, but subordination did not require that he be debased. Conservative whites talked a great deal about the low social position of the Negro; they also talked much of raising him by education and example.

Nor did the Bourbons act to deny the suffrage to the Negro. For more than two decades after Reconstruction Negroes continued to vote, although, because of local pressures and tricky election laws, in reduced numbers. In part the Bourbon acquiescence in this situation reflected a general white reluctance to invite the return of Northern power by tampering with voting rights. But in larger part the ruling whites accepted Negro suffrage because they wanted it that way. As the vote of a propertyless class, it was something to be watched and kept in hand. But as the vote of an inferior and inert people, it was something that could be manipulated for the benefit of the rich whites, the only class that had the means to do the manipulating. "As the negro becomes more intelligent," observed planter leader Wade Hampton, "he naturally allies himself with the more conservative of the whites."

White direction of the Negro vote took various forms, some simple and crass, others subtle and complex. Ironically, on occasion the Bourbons turned the Negroes against the Republicans. In a Louisiana Congressional election in 1884 one local leader outlined for the sugar planters how they could defeat the Republican candidate. Let owners and managers tell the Negro workers to vote for the Democrat, he advised: "They naturally receive with deference the expression of opinion by their employer on all subjects. . . . Nearly all the leading colored men are with us and they need only the offer of substantial moral support from the employers to swell the number of the supporters of Mr. Gay from the ranks of the colored employees."

Sometimes, as when two white factions competed for the colored vote, the manipulation was as blunt as violence. Such a situation in a Louisiana parish was described by a man who helped to resolve it: "I helped the Charlie Thompson crowd vote the negro, carried a Winchester in aid of his right to vote, and assisted in precipitating a campaign of riot and blood-shed such as had not been witnessed in St. Landry since the war. The riot of 1868 was white against black—that of 1895 and 1896 was white man against white man, for the Negro vote. One side said, 'He should not vote. If he does we go under.' The other side said, 'He must vote. He will save us.' "

Usually the tactics were much more artful. Perhaps the smoothest working example of co-operation between upperclass whites and Negroes was seen in Mississippi. Here there was, if not an open deal, certainly an understood agreement between the contracting parties. The whites stipulated to help secure federal patronage for the Negroes and to support the colored politicians against white rivals in the Republican party. In return, the Negro leaders pledged to deliver a number of votes to the Bourbons in state and local elections—enough to keep the conservatives in control. The arrangement extended down to a division of local offices. Commonly the whites would agree with the Negro leaders to assign so many offices to Negro Democrats, usually minor ones but sometimes including seats in the legislature. The allocation of places to Negroes was particularly prevalent in the Negro counties of the Delta. Exactly opposite to what Will Percy thought it had been, Negroes served in county offices after Reconstruction—indeed, may have held more of them than in the day of the carpetbagger. By devices such as the ones described and by others as well the Bourbons faced down every threat to their place until the storm of Populism burst on the land in the 1890's.

Lately it has been the fashion to deride the Populists: to say that in both the South and the West the movement was not a genuine class protest, that it was essentially superficial because directed against such outside "devils" as Eastern and European bankers, that it was even an expression of incipient Fascism. As far back as 1941, W. J. Cash dismissed Southern Populism as representing no serious internal division in the section but only a groping toward class awareness on the part of the masses. Now doubtless some liberal historians have made far too much of Populism.

For one thing, its strength has been exaggerated; it never gave any real promise of developing into even a formidable third party. For another, it was not nearly so radical as the inflamed vocabulary of many of its spokesmen, especially in the South, seemed to indicate. But to say that Populism lacked realism because it blamed everything on outside enemies, the bankers, is to miss the fact that the farmers in this first stage of protest were naturally naive in economic matters. To charge that because the Populists sometimes referred to Jewish bankers they were Fascists in the making is to mistake enduring but essentially harmless habits of the American mind for the real thing. And to shunt off Southern Populism as having little meaning or effect is to ignore much of what happened as well as to place too academic an interpretation on politics.

By any standards the South was the strongest center of Populism. Southern Populists were more radical than their

Western allies, more ready to espouse fundamental changes in the economic system and less willing to accept palliatives like free silver. They were more stubbornly insistent on maintaining basic principles, on retaining their party identity, on resisting absorption by the Democrats. Perhaps they were so uncompromising because they had had to contend against forces far more implacable than anything faced by the Westerners—economic and social pressures, charges of racial treason, election frauds, and outright violence. Southern Populism collided full tilt with the whole edifice of Southern politics; with the romantic attachment to images of the past; with the separation of politics and economics; with the entombing one-party system; and with the folk unity forged by Reconstruction. The Populists talked the language of economics and self-interest. They spoke of class consciousness and class legislation, of combining farmers and laborers and sections in one party, of using government to solve economic problems. Most alarming of all, they said that economic self-interest transcended race. They proposed to fit the Negro in somewhere in their great combination.

Of all the Populist spokesmen, the one who gave the fullest and frankest expression of the primacy of class interests over race was Georgia's Tom Watson. Over and over he stressed that the poor white man and the poor colored man were caught in the same economic trap and could save themselves only by working together. "You are made to hate each other," he told the races, "because upon that hatred is rested the keystone of the arch of financial despotism which enslaves you both. You are deceived and blinded that you may not see how this race antagonism perpetuates a money system which beggars you both." With the dogmatism of the true doctrinaire, Watson was certain that awareness of interest would unite the races under the banner of Populism. "Gratitude may fail; so may sympathy, and friendship, and generosity, and patriotism, but, in the long run, self-interest always controls," he proclaimed. "Let it once appear plainly that it is to the interest of the colored man to vote with the white man and he will do it."

To implement the principles announced by Watson and other party theorists the Populists put into their platforms provisions supporting the Negro's right to vote and hold office and denouncing the convict lease system and lynching. At Populist gatherings there was always some kind of symbolic recognition of the rights of Negro members. When at a national convention it was proposed to nominate a Negro for assistant secretary, the Southern delegates roared approval, and a Georgian rose to assure: "I wish to say that we can stand that down in Georgia."

The Populist leaders were undoubtedly sincere in their professions for racial co-operation. But from their statements it is easy to draw, as some writers have done, unwarranted conclusions. There was much more talk about co-operation than actual accomplishment. While Negroes were welcomed to Populist rallies and meetings, they generally participated in a minor and segregated capacity. The mass body of Populists might listen respectfully to the exhortations of men like Watson, but in their hearts they were as committed to racial concepts as their class had always been. And here was the strategic problem that the Populists could never surmount. The people to whom they made their strongest appeal, the farmers, cherished stronger feelings on race than any other group in the South.

During Reconstruction and after, the conservative or rich whites, with greater material and political means, had tried to introduce a plurality of issues into politics and had failed and had ended by embracing and exploiting the one great issue; and where the conservatives

had failed, the Populists, with lesser skills, were not likely
to succeed. Possibly the Populists could have found no
way out of the dilemma, but their tactics were calculated
to bring almost certain failure. They attacked a deep-
seated problem with a too-simple formula, the self-
interest of classes. More serious, they attacked frankly
and openly, labeling the problem and themselves as the
solvers. A more realistic or cynical operator might have
suggested that a better approach would be to treat the
problem without talking about it.

But even when all the factors militating against the
Populists are listed—the obstacles thrown up by their
enemies and their own omissions of procedure—it is a
matter of some amazement and a fact of profound historical importance that they had as much success as they
did. They won a number of state and local elections and
saw some that they won stolen from them. In the Louisiana election of 1896, for example, the Democrats carried
only five of the twenty-five parishes with a white majority
but won the state by sweeping the parishes with a heavy
black population. Bossier parish, where there were ten
Negro voters to one white, delivered a majority of 2,500
to the Democrats. It was freely admitted that in some parishes the returns were liberally doctored to ensure a
Democratic victory. The same methods were used in
other states, and the Democrats did not mind boasting
about how they won. Said Governor William C. Oates of
Alabama: "I told them to go to it, boys, count them out.
We had to do it."

Some observers noted a beautiful irony in the situation. The party that had overthrown the corruption of
Reconstruction and established white supremacy was
maintaining itself in power by fraud and Negro votes.
But the Populists could play the same game and did. In-
creasingly they wooed the Negro vote, even, as they be-

came more desperate, entering into coalitions with the Republicans. The result was to inaugurate a carnival of fraud and to prepare the downfall of Populism. The spectacle of white factions competing openly for the colored vote, with the Republicans and the national government hovering ominously in the background, was genuinely frightening to many people. If nothing else had killed off the Populists, this alone would have done it.

Many factors were responsbile for the ultimate passing of Populism, both as a national and as a sectional force. Perhaps the best explanation is the one that encompasses all others—the Populists simply suffered the fate of all promising American third parties, absorption by one of the major parties. But the failure of Southern Populism, of the mood more than the movement, resulted from particular factors peculiar to the South itself. These were several and cumulative, but Tom Watson, the ablest and frankest spokesman of the Southerners, looking back in later years was sure that one issue alone had killed Populism. It was, in his words, the inevitable "nigger." The doctrine of self-interest had collapsed when confronted with the cry of race, Watson concluded sadly. A Populist might fill the ears of a white tenant with economic arguments; but when somebody came along and shouted Negro rule, "the entire fabric of reason and common sense which you had patiently constructed would fall, and the poor tenant would joyously hug the chain of an actual wretchedness rather than do any experimenting on a question of mere sentiment."

Bitterly Watson depicted the influence of the Negro on his own career: "Consider the advantage of position that Bryan had over me. His field of work was the plastic, restless and growing West; mine was the hide-bound, rock-ribbed Bourbon South. *Besides, Bryan had no everlasting and overshadowing Negro Question to hamper and handicap his progress. I HAD.*" Watson, who had once stood forth as a champion of Negro rights, who had demanded suffrage for the Negro as for any citizen, finally came to advocate a new strategy—the only way to eliminate the Negro issue in politics was to eliminate the Negro from politics. Let the Negroes be disfranchised, and then the whites could divide freely on all questions, could vote for a plurality of issues instead of one. Many Southerners, not always for the same reasons, reached the same conclusion.

The provisions or the devices of the disfranchising laws enacted by Southern legislatures in the 1890's are so well known as not to require elaboration. So also are the restrictions of the segregation or Jim Crow acts which began to appear on the books in the late eighties and which were constantly expanded until shortly after 1900. We know a great deal about the nature of these first attempts by the South to place the Negro in a place of legal or formal inferiority, but much research remains to be done on the men and the forces that produced the laws. Certainly there would seem to be more than coincidence in the passage of the segregation laws at the same time that the farmers' movement was making its power felt in state politics; the acts clearly reflected the racial concepts that had animated the rural white masses since the beginning of Reconstruction. "In fact," notes Professor Woodward, "an increase of Jim Crow laws upon the statute books of a state is almost an accurate index of the decline of the reactionary regimes of the Redeemers and the triumph of white democratic movements."

The social and human impulses behind the disfranchising laws are not so patent. These acts were enacted when the Populist movement was at its crest or just over it and were obviously an outgrowth of the deep divisions aroused by Populism. The available evidence indicates that the impetus for disfranchisement came from farmer leaders like Ben Tillman of South Carolina, who had embraced some of the ideals of Populism but who had remained in the Democratic party. The motivation of such men is plain. Driving to gain ascendancy in the Democratic organization, they could please the race-conscious farmers by depriving the Negro of the vote and at the same time deprive the Bourbons of a potent weapon against the farmers.

Tillman did not mind bragging how disfranchisement had been accomplished, either to other Southerners or to Northerners. On the floor of the United States Senate he said: "We took the government away. We stuffed ballot boxes. We shot them. We are not ashamed of it." Nor was he above conceding that some of the laws, notably the "understanding" clause, had to be administered unfairly to disqualify Negroes without taking in whites. The understanding clause he described as "the most charming piece of mechanism ever invented." Perhaps there was a little fraud in it, but "some poisons in small doses" were "very salutary and valuable medicines. . . . I only swallow enough of it to protect the ballot of the poor white men."

But while the farmer chiefs led off the movement, the rich whites seem to have gone along willingly and even in some states to have taken over control. They acted largely out of a desire to placate the masses after the upheavals of Populism; as after Reconstruction, there was a general feeling among the whites that the ranks should be closed. Again, the competition for colored votes by two white factions had shot the prices demanded by the voters up to new highs. It was simply becoming too expensive to buy up a Negro majority. As somebody observed, the South had to take the vote away from the Negro to keep the white politicians from stealing it. The hand of the Bour-

bons in the disfranchising laws was clearly apparent in
the language of some of the provisions, so drafted as to
disqualify the poorest whites as well as the Negroes. Indeed, some conservatives proclaimed in words almost identical with those of their predecessors in Reconstruction
that poor men of any color did not deserve the ballot.
"The true philosophy of the movement," explained one
conservative, "was to establish restricted suffrage, and to
place the power of government in the hands of the intelligent and virtuous." Not all white men were supposed to
participate in the free debate on all issues after the
removal of the Negro from politics.

Almost as Populism passed from the scene, another
movement arrived, appearing in all sections and known
in all as Progressivism. There was an obvious continuity
in the two movements, and a measure of ideological sim-
ilarity. Both were nourished in the same soil, the fears
and tensions engendered by the rise of big business, and
both proposed in some way or other to attack bigness
and restore the economic position of the ordinary man.
But whereas Populism had represented a kind of frantic
threshing around by desperate farmers, Progressivism had
more of a middle-class and urban tone; it stood for
moderate reforms of the economy, and it avoided both
the extreme program and the extreme rhetoric of revolution that had scared off many people from Populism.
Progressive leaders were likely to be lawyers, editors, even
businessmen, rather than farmers, and they spoke a language that should have alarmed nobody.

This was the structure of Progressivism on the national
level, but the Southern version was pretty much the same.
Below the Potomac there were more Progressive leaders
from the farmer class, some of them, like Tillman, hang-
ing over from the agrarian unrest of the nineties and
merging easily into the new movement. But the South

could also display its urban Progressives, like Hoke Smith of Georgia; and its business Progressives, like Braxton Comer of Alabama. Whatever their origins, Southern Progressives advocated a common program. They talked of controlling the big corporations, enlarging appropriations for education, establishing agricultural schools, in short, of doing much the same things that Northern Progressives were doing. All this seemed to herald a new kind of politics for the South—a more realistic kind that recognized the relation between politics and economics. Perhaps those who had said that from white solidarity on one issue would come white division on many issues had been right.

It would not turn out that way at all, and for many reasons. Some of these were rooted deep in the South's history, in its conservative aversion to change and suspicion of that which was new, in its preoccupation with dream images and attachment to romanticism. But some were special to the social context that had made Progressivism possible. In the first place, the argument used to carry disfranchisement, that the whites must unite to divide, had an effect opposite to that intended. The *mystique* of unity became a force in itself, resulting in what was almost a third legend to add to the Lost Cause and the Old South. Southern intellectuals talked seriously and sincerely of "the unity of race" as a proper basis of political life, of the relation between political and social solidarity, of the advantages of racial distinctions over those of class. The politicians might not understand all the language of the intellectuals, but they grasped completely the practical implications. Second, Southern Progressives were, as they had to be, Democrats. They had to operate in a one-party system that in itself would have acted as a restriction on division but that was doubly confining now, because with the memories of Populism still fresh no politician would dare to press an issue to the point where he could be accused of disrupting the white man's party.

But the principal reason for the fading of the high hopes of Progressivism was that the race issue would not disappear, that it remained on the scene to dominate all of politics. It did not disappear because the politicians would not let it go; it was too good a weapon to lose. Many a Progressive reformer—for example, Hoke Smith, Josephus Daniels, Carter Glass—went into office on a white-supremacy platform, and as many others exploited racism to increase their power. Commonly in a campaign of the Progressive period the discussion of economic questions would be shunted aside if one or another of the candidates introduced the Negro business, either to give himself an issue or to deprive his opponent of one; then the air rang with warnings against the black menace.

If much of this sounds like flogging a dead horse, it was. The career of Hoke Smith affords a classic example of the course of the Southern Progressive. Beginning as a conservative, Smith turned to Progressivism, and in 1905 offered for governor on a platform stressing regulation of the railroads. When he had been a Bourbon, he had held moderate views on race relations. He had advocated a generous paternalism on the part of the whites to raise the Negroes up, had supported Negro education, and had condemned lynching. Probably when he entered the campaign he did not intend to emphasize the race question, but when his foes attacked his railroad program and hinted that he was soft on white supremacy, he seized the issue and ran off with it. "No more important question can be presented to the people of Georgia than the disfranchisement of the ignorant, purchasable negro vote," he thundered. "This is a white man's country. . . . No matter how secure we may feel at present from negro domination, if . . . there is danger to the state at large, or to any county or community in Georgia from this curse, it will be folly for us to neglect any means within our power to remove the danger."

The campaign developed into a shouting contest between two white factions, each one seeking to outdo the other in promising the maintenance of white supremacy. One Negro leader could not help wondering what the tumult was all about, since the Negroes were practically disfranchised already. There may have been design in what happened. Some observers thought that the railroads had deliberately promoted the diversion. "Now it happened that in the progress of the campaign," said the Atlanta *Journal,* "the political managers, whose slogan was, 'Let well enough alone,' found themselves most vulnerable on the railroad question. The facts and the arguments were all with the people's candidate. So the attempt was made to shift the issue from the main one to the minor one of negro disfranchisement."

If Southern Progressivism never seemed to get off the ground, so to speak, it was not just because of the obfuscations engendered by racism. Rather, it was that Progressive leaders failed in their program and in their persons to satisfy the aspirations and needs of the people. In some states a respectable number of laws were enacted, but although this legislation corrected some inequalities and embodied some of the latest features of reform, it did not touch or impress the most submerged classes. Summarizing the end effect of Ben Tillman's movement, Professor Francis B. Simkins writes: "There had been no material improvement, no spiritual awakening, real or illusory. Tillman lacked the fervor or the fanaticism of the great evangelist. He had aroused certain classes without satisfying them. The tenant farmers and the small landowners were hopping the same clods they had hopped

before they heard of Tillman." Southern Progressivism
was too conservative and conventional, too withdrawn,
really, to appeal to the masses. Essentially romantic, it
often did no more than to identify social and economic
evils with a vague aggregation of enemies called the
North or Northern business interest.

Nor did Progressive leaders compensate for their omissions of accomplishment by furnishing in their own persons any vicarious release for the frustrations of the
masses. That is, the Progressive representation of leadership did not provide the psychological outlets that a rural
and a poor people craved and needed: a sense of identification with their spokesmen; a feeling that however
drab their life or despised their estate they were somehow expressing themselves through these spokesmen,
were through them flinging defiance at their enemies; an
assurance that because their chiefs were swaggering char-
acters who told the mighty where to head in, they were
pretty hell-for-leather fellows themselves. Only a few of
the Progressives, notably Tillman and James K. Vardaman, spoke the language the masses wanted to hear. They
loved it when Tillman expounded on his peculiarities,
perhaps seeing an image of themselves: "Some of you expected to see hoofs and horns. . . . I have some peculiarities. . . . I'm what I am, and God made me what I am, and
therefore, if this conglomeration of flesh and bones becomes a factor in South Carolina, it will be by reason of
the peculiarities with which my creator endowed me. I
am lefthanded, and have written with my left paw. I am
one-eyed. Some say I can see more with that one eye than
some men can see with a dozen."

By a natural order of succession that seems to puzzle
observers like Professor Woodward the Progressives were
followed by leaders of a new type. After Tillman in South
Carolina came Cole Blease, and after Vardaman in Mis-

sissippi, Theodore Bilbo. The Bleases and the Bilbos are the men called in the history books, although the term is rarely defined, the demagogues. There is no mystery about their ascent to power. They came, they conquered because they gave the masses something that was perhaps not fundamentally important but that nobody else was prepared to give. As W. J. Cash shrewdly perceived, they were primarily interested in place, in jobs. They challenged the conservative hierarchies but made no sustained effort to destroy them. They built their own machines but only to perpetuate themselves in office, and hence could not raise up a new succession. They did not put forward programs, even of the modest variety of the Progressives. What, then, did they offer? What explains their appeal? Very simply, they made the masses feel important, they stroked the ego of democracy. They voiced the frustrations and the resentments of the submerged classes that had been stirred but not satisfied by Populism and Progressivism. They denounced in savage diatribes those who they assured the people were their enemies—the Yankees, the Negroes, the patricians—and the people, seeing in all this a representation of themselves in action against their oppressors, mistook the rhetoric of victory for the reality.

The great wonder of it all was that out of the sound and the fury nothing happened. The demagogues posed far less of a threat to the established order than the Progressives. In this respect, a comparison between Tillman and Blease is instructive. Blease seemed to be more radical than his predecessor. He employed an even more violent language, and he drew into his ranks an even more depressed group than the farmers, the mill workers, excluded by Tillman as "the damned factory class." But Blease offered these people no program of betterment, and he consistently opposed and defeated legislation to benefit labor. Yet the very people that he undercut cherished him as their champion. It has been said that Blease's great contribution to Southern politics was his ability "to make a class appeal without offering a class program." Professor Simkins, who tends to look fondly on Southern resistance to change, thinks that the politics represented by Blease was all the Southern people wanted. He writes: "Blease, despite the violence of his language, was not as radical as Tillman. He was too devoted to the South Carolina tradition to approve progressive ideas. If Tillman's program of reform lacked comprehensiveness, Blease scarcely had any program whatever. Yet he voiced the feelings of the common people in their own language and made them think he was one of them. . . . This satisfied the ordinary man more completely than a program of social reform." Perhaps so, but not forever and not in every Southern state would the ordinary man be content with this most recent personification of romantic politics.

LECTURE

FOUR

The Politics of the Longs

ONCE HUEY LONG WAS ASKED IF HE SAW ANY RESEMBLANCE between himself and Hitler. His reaction was immediate, blunt, and revealing. "Don't compare me to that so-and-so," he bellowed. "Anybody that lets his public policies be mixed up with religious prejudice is a plain God-damned fool." He touched on the theme of religion in politics on another occasion. In 1934 the Ku Klux Klan, or some of its representatives, attacked him and his program. He hoped not to be drawn into a fight on grounds of the Klan's choosing. "I have always avoided any religious fight," he said, "for the sake of the good I have tried to do for everybody. I have never stepped aside to denounce a Klansman or anti-Klansman, always hoping to have all of the people understand what I was trying to do and to help me in that effort." As it turned out, in the Klan business he would have to denounce somebody, and none other than the head Klansman, Dr. Hiram Evans, who threatened to campaign against Long in Louisiana. Long issued a public statement reflecting unmistakably on the Imperial Wizard's ancestry and pledging that he would never set foot in Louisiana.

But Long did not speak out until, in effect, he was forced to by a voiced threat to his position. His reluctance did not spring from any lack of courage, for many times he would demonstrate that he possessed ample amounts of political courage and audacity. Rather, it was that he did not want to get involved in a controversy over questions which in his view were false or unreal issues. The implications of his statements quoted above are fascinating. Religion had no place in politics, not because it was intolerant or un-American to inject it, but because in politics an issue of religion was unimportant, because a discussion of religion sidetracked the issues that were important. In Long's thinking the only issues that mattered, the only issues that were real were ones concerning power and economics. Early in his career he set his sights on definite goals—the erection of a power structure without parallel in American government and the enactment of a politico-economic program positively undreamed of in Southern politics—and during his short but explosive life he moved relentlessly toward his goals, always sublimating what he considered irrelevant issues, whether of race or religion. He is the supreme example in recent Southern politics of the coldly realistic operator. His successors in the enduring faction he created in the Louisiana Democratic party would follow the general outlines of the strategy he laid down, although varying their tactics to fit new situations. They would face forces of opposition that in some ways were more intensive than those of his day, and they would record achievements that were as remarkable as his.

In the years after Reconstruction the pattern of politics in Louisiana was broadly similar to that of other Southern states. A hierarchy representing the upper-income classes emerged to grasp the sources of power. The Louisiana hierarchy exhibited the usual elements present in a Bourbon or conservative power structure plus some peculiar to the local scene. In addition to the usual planting interests, there were important business groups: lumber, sugar, railroads; and centered in New Orleans shipping, gas, and electrical concerns. Eventually overshadowing all the business factions was oil. In the 1920's the Standard Oil Company became a major economic and political force in the life of the state. Last, there was what could not be found any other place in the South, a genuine big city machine. This was the organization known as the Old Regulars or the Choctaw Club that reigned in New Orleans in alliance with the city's business and financial powers. The Old Regular machine performed much the same functions, desirable and undesirable, as city machines in the North, and it carried elections by much the same techniques. Old Regular bosses were accustomed to boasting that as late as the night before an election they could arrange to throw enough votes to carry any contest. Usually in a gubernatorial election the machine would endorse a candidate with a strong country following in return for a pledge of control over state patronage in the city.

Such then was the Louisiana hierarchy, conservative in make-up and outlook, devoted to the past and satisfied with the present, dedicated to the protection of privilege, and staidly corrupt. For fifty years after Reconstruction it ruled almost without challenge. Populism offered only a brief threat before subsiding, and no demagogue of the Tillman type appeared to advance even mild reforms. There was not even a Blease to demand some of the places reserved for members of the oligarchy.

It was upon this serene scene that Huey Long burst like a bombshell in the 1920's, and thereafter things would never be the same. Long came from Winn parish in the north-central part of the state. Winn was undeniably, in the economic sense, a poor parish, featuring small farms, cutover timber lands, and lumber mills. It would be a mistake, however, to suppose, as practically all writers of the popular school who have written about the Longs have, that the family was abjectly poor or trashy or without culture. The Longs were of a familiar Southern type —middle-class hill farmers, proud, independent, with a respect for learning and often a pathetic desire to acquire it. Practically every so-called demagogue emerged from precisely such a background. The Longs were economically a cut above the average in Winn, and every member of the large family received some kind of college education.

Winn parish did have, however, a historical heritage different from most Southern communities. In 1861 the delegate from the parish opposed secession, and the mass of the people displayed a feeling toward the Confederate adventure that was more than cool; the consensus seemed to be that this was a rich man's war and let the rich fight it. Later Winn became the center of Populist strength in the state, and after the demise of Populism a surprisingly strong Socialist party emerged, representing a rural brand of Socialism, to be sure, but still bearing a label not customarily worn in the rural South.

There is an obvious relation between Long's environment and his political thought. The program he would advocate was a later version of Populism. But was his strong sense of realism a product of the unrelieved starkness of Winn parish or of something in his inner self? We cannot know. But it is of great significance that in his entire career he never seriously mentioned the two great Southern legends, the Old South and the Lost Cause. At a time when most politicians attempted to assuage the misery of the masses by spinning tales of past glories—the lovely South before Sumter, Jeb Stuart's dancing plume,

the boys in gray plunging up the slopes at Gettysburg—
Huey Long talked about economics and the present and
the future.

After a spectacular career on the Public Service Com-
mission, where he made a name attacking the big oil
companies, Long ran for governor in 1924. He failed, ran
again in 1928 and was elected, and then proceeded to re-
make completely the political pattern of the state. Before
his advent on the scene governors were elected by "leaders," who were usually the sheriffs of the parishes. The
successful candidate was the one who could line up the
largest number of country leaders and then make a deal
with the New Orleans machine. Abruptly, rudely, and
with a great deal of zest, Long erased this arrangement.
In his two gubernatorial campaigns he would often in-
vade a local area and attack the boss. There was calculated design in this. He knew that in some cases he could
not get the boss's support anyway, but more often he did
not care. He was out to break the power of the leaders by
going over their heads to the voters. For the first time a
candidate for governor systematically stumped the whole
state, and for the first time the masses, the people at the
forks of the creeks, heard a candidate appeal to them for
support and promise a program designed to benefit them.
The comparative ease with which Long succeeded demon-
strates that the masses were waiting for such a leader.
"Overnight, one might say, the leaders found themselves
without followers," said one almost incredulous opponent,
"and the mob was in control."

Long then proceeded to create his own state and
local organization. On the parish level he was always care-
ful to name a committee of leaders, instead of having just
one. His purpose here was, as intimates frankly and ad-
miringly admit, to prevent one man from becoming too
powerful. With several leaders, each one would watch the

others, and all would compete to exercise dividend authority. "He cut out the middleman in politics," said one associate. "That's a system you can't beat." It is a mark of Long's artistry as a student of power that sometimes in a parish where he had a large popular following, enough to carry a state election, he would leave an anti-Long sheriff in office—to prevent his own leaders from becoming too powerful and to keep them hungry for future victories. But if Long had stopped with forging a machine of his own, no matter how elaborate and effective, he would have merely followed the course of previous popular leaders, and would have met the same frustrating fate. He went a long step farther.

As W. J. Cash was probably the first to notice, Long was the first Southern demagogue, or to use a more satisfactory term, the first mass leader to set himself, not to bring the established machine to terms, but to overwhelm it and replace it with one of his own. In the words of V. O. Key: "He did not permit himself, in an oft-repeated pattern, to be hamstrung by a legislature dominated by old hands experienced in legislation and frequently under corporate retainer. He elected his own legislatures and erected a structure of political power both totalitarian and terrifying." When Long first went into office, he took with him only a minority of pledged supporters in the legislature. His immediate problem was to create an organization to pass his legislative program. In the lower chamber he could count on only nineteen votes whereas, as many of his measures had to be cast in the shape of constitutional amendments, he needed a two-thirds majority or sixty-seven. It was the same problem that had frustrated other liberal governors of the period, in both the South and the North. Blocked by their legislatures, they ended up by coming to terms with the opposition or by dissipating their energies in impotent crusades for sham issues.

Huey Long encountered his reverses, but defeat only intensified his determination to win through to his objectives. In fact, the techniques employed by the opposition, which sometimes included the crassest kinds of material pressures, and the violence of the reactions against him, which often took the form of fighting a bill merely because he had proposed it, had the effect of making him more fiercely implacable and of driving him to greater excesses in the use of power than otherwise would have been the case. Eventually he built up a disciplined majority in the legislature. The cost was high. In the frank words of one associate: "They all didn't come for free." Again, the process illustrates Long's sheer artistry as a manipulator of power.

The basis of his structure was patronage. First, he extended his control over existing boards and departments, and then through the constant creations of new agencies to perform new functions he continually enlarged the patronage at his disposal. That is, the job well did not dry up after the first distribution but always remained full. Finally Long was able to deprive the opposition of almost all political sustenance and to bring even the New Orleans machine to its knees. In 1935 in a radio address he said that when he ran for governor in 1928, the opposition was fighting for "our ground." Now, he announced grimly: "We are fighting for their ground. They say today they want peace. Well, they'll get peace when they get peaceful." At the end he was preparing to fit all pieces of the Democratic party into his organization. The opposition would have a place and would receive the rewards suitable to its role, but Long would determine both the place and the rewards. Not even the most gifted political operators of other times or other sections had thought in such daring terms or envisioned a machine so powerful.

Perhaps the most remarkable feature of the Long power structure—it was unique in Southern politics—was its material basis, or, put in blunter words, the techniques used by the organization to raise the money to sustain itself and to perform the welfare functions expected of machines in the pre-New Deal era. The Long organization did not ask for money or promise anything in return for contributions. It demanded and took what it needed, and was in effect self-sustaining. During Long's administration the state undertook a vast road building program. The road contractors and contractors on other public works were assessed for regular contributions in elections; so also were the distributors of highway machinery and the companies that wrote the state's insurance. For obviously good reasons all these interests met their obligations. The number of state employees was deliberately maintained at a high level, the jobs being spread around lavishly, and the holders had to contribute a percentage of their salaries to the machine campaign fund. Some of the top officials had to render monthly payments, but in Long's time lower salaried workers were assessed only before elections. In addition, there were approximately a thousand men, leaders and beneficiaries, who stood ready to supply money for emergency needs such as paying up poll taxes or covering the accounts of officials who had been tempted off the narrow path. Surviving Long leaders will frankly detail these financial manipulations. Not only that, they will insist passionately that the organization's methods of raising money were moral, and certainly more moral than the methods of the opposition. The opposition, and for that matter machines in other states, they say, went to corporate interests and asked for money under the table and hence were subject to some kind of control. But the Long machine exacted money openly and was accountable only to itself and to the voters.

During Long's lifetime the charge was flung freely at him, in Louisiana and out, that he was a dictator, a Mussolini of the bayous, a Hitler of the swamps, and the label has survived to the present. In liberal intellectual circles today it is fashionable to dismiss Long as an American Fascist. The appellation may serve the purpose of those who use it, either as a convenient smear or as a substitute for serious analysis, but as a designation it is inaccurate and offers no explanation of the phenomenon of Huey Long. The trouble with the dictator or Fascist tag is that it has a European connotation and does not fit the realities of the American political scene. Whatever Long was, he was completely American and Southern and wholly native in his outlook and methods. He was, in the most descriptive phrase, an American boss. The only respect in which he differed from the familiar pattern of the boss was in his concept of power—his genius in devising power devices and his ruthless readiness to employ power to attain his ends. Most American politicians have been reluctant to use power, or, when they have used it, to admit what they were doing. But Long openly exulted in his power and was remarkably frank in explaining his exercise of it. He fits the image of the politician of "ambition and talents" that Abraham Lincoln once warned against, although in the unconscious admiration of his account Lincoln may have been projecting himself into the role: "Towering genius disdains a beaten path. It seeks regions hitherto unexplored. It sees *no distinction* in adding story to story, upon monuments of fame, erected to the memory of others. . . . It scorns to tread in the footsteps of *any* predecessor, however illustrious. It thirsts and burns for distinction; and, if possible, it will have it. . . ."

The most sensational demonstration of Long's power techniques came when as United States Senator but still boss of the state he returned to Louisiana to operate the legislature. Special session after special session was called at his command. He would dominate committee hearings and storm into the chamber of either house while in session to shout directions at his cohorts. Laws were jammed through at a rate never witnessed in a legislative body. On one occasion forty-four bills were passed in twenty-two minutes. In seven special sessions between August 1934 and September 1935 a total of 463 bills was enacted. Some bills started out as one thing in one house and were amended to something entirely different in the other, without the opposition or most of his followers realizing what had happened. The exhibition horrified many observers. But the travesty on the legislative process was not as bad as it seemed. Before every day's meeting Long held a closed caucus of his people and went over every proposed bill in detail, and while he was adamant on general principles there was a measure of discussion and criticism. Moreover, many of his measures had to be cast as constitutional amendments and submitted to a popular vote. Thus fourteen amendments passed in one session were ratified by the voters by a margin of seven to one.

But even when these extenuations are made, one has to wonder if Long's methods comported with the spirit of democratic government. The interesting thing is that Long, a surprisingly introspective politician, wondered too, in fact, wondered about his whole role and his place in the historical process of which he was a part. "They say they don't like my methods," he once said in an address. "Well, I don't like them either. . . . I'd much rather get up before a legislature and say 'Now this is a good law; it's for the benefit of the people, and I'd like for you to vote for it in the interest of the public welfare.'

Only I know that laws ain't made that way. You've got to fight fire with fire." There is some terrible sense of urgency in the psychology of politicians who are driven by a sense of mission, a gnawing fear that time may be running out on them. Associates and members of his family attest that Long was always oppressed by time. To one man who asked why he ran bills through the legislature so fast Long replied: "You sometimes fight fire with fire. The means justify the end. I would do it some other way if there was time or if it wasn't necessary to do it this way."

Running through all his justifications of his course is the theme that he had to resort to extreme and even brutal methods; the phrase of fighting fire with fire appears again and again. It is almost impossible to separate the factors that made up his thinking on the subject of power, to say which were real and which were rationalization. The thesis most often advanced to explain him, that he simply illustrates Acton's dictum of the corrupting effects of power, is not enough. He was fascinated with power and its uses, and undoubtedly toward the end he had become so accustomed to the exercise of power, to the very convenience of it, that he could not give it up.

But there is more to the story. Epitomized in Long's life is a personal and also a sectional tragedy. When he first entered office, he exhibited many of the traits of the typical liberal reformer, including a somewhat idealistic concept of human nature and the nature of politics. But the unrelenting and sometimes unreasoning opposition he encountered and the constant attempts of his foes to destroy him, especially the try at impeachment in 1929, changed him. There was something almost wistful in his description of how he had lived out his entire career under some kind of threat of forced removal from office: "I have tried for about sixteen years to have it some other way, and it has never been any other way, so now I have stopped trying to have it any other way." After the failure of impeachment he became harder and more cynical. He resolved that thereafter he would so strengthen and solidify his position that no similar attempt could succeed in the future. But as he drove toward always greater goals of power he never lost completely the fear that the old hierarchy might recuperate and block him or possibly unseat him. Perhaps the gravest indictment that can be made of conservative Southern politics is that it forced leaders like Long to become ruthless operators of power. But, it is significant to note, as with other aspects of his position, Long wondered about his power structure. As invincible as he had made it, he apparently thought that it could be only temporary because he repeatedly warned the men who would be his successors that they could not exercise his authority without tragic results.

But no matter how adept Long was in the arts of power, he could never have sustained himself or his organization merely by manipulation. He had a program. He promised something, and he delivered it. Long was the first Southern mass leader to leave aside race baiting and appeals to the Southern tradition and the Southern past and address himself to the social and economic problems of the present. He promised big, partly because that was his nature and partly because a big promise that took in the interest of large numbers was good strategy. "Do not ever," he advised, "put one of those Mother Hubbard things out that is going to accommodate just one percent."

In a short space his record can only be summarized. When he became governor, Louisiana had 296 miles of concrete roads, 35 miles of asphalt roads, 5,728 miles of gravel roads, and three major bridges within the state highway system. By 1935 the figures read: 2,446 miles of concrete roads, 1,308 miles of asphalt roads, 9,629 miles of gravel roads, and more than forty major bridges within the highway system. In the field of education, free textbooks were provided, causing a twenty per cent jump in school enrollment; appropriations for higher education were increased; and over 100,000 adult illiterates, of both races, were enrolled in free night schools. Facilities in state hospitals and institutions were enlarged, and the services were modernized and humanized. Just as important as the material accomplishments was the impact of Huey Long on the psychology of the state. He created a new consciousness of government on the part of the masses and thereby revitalized state politics. By advancing issues that mattered and by repealing the poll tax, he stirred voter interest to a height unmatched in any other Southern state, and he left Louisiana with an enduring bifactionalism that has many of the attributes of a two-party system.

When people in Louisiana try to describe the impact of Long and his movement, they have trouble in putting their thoughts into words. They are obviously deeply moved, but they are embarrassed that they may sound emotional or exaggerated. Thus one associate telling the writer of Long's advent in politics said: "To run for office you had either to be indorsed by the sugar barons, the banks, or the railroads. Without them putting their hands on you and anointing you, you were beyond the pale. . . . And the very fact that he was able to become governor of this state without the titular rulers—they never forgave him for that. And as a result he brought the state out of the mud, gave them free school books, and hospitals. It sounds like a political speech, but if those things had not been done this state would have lagged behind until it was pushed into it by mass hysteria." Jonathan

Daniels recounts a conversation with a businessman of French descent in the Cajun country. This man told Daniels that Louisiana "was the back door to China before Huey Long came. . . . Huey Long changed Louisiana from a hell hole to a paradise. He was emancipator. He brought light." Then he quoted Huey as saying: "Many are walking. Some are buggy riding. Some are in automobiles. But I'm flying." Perhaps Long had pushed too hard, this observer conceded with the realism common to many Latins: "Maybe we moved too fast in the last eight years; certainly we moved too slowly for centuries before that."

A perceptive New Orleans lawyer with a detached interest in politics went to great lengths to impress on the writer the nature of the Long appeal to the masses. Although he had never been a member of the Long organization, he agreed to run for a state office on the Long ticket shortly after Huey's death. Before, he had thought that the Longs won elections because they made demagogic speeches or manipulated the vote. But when he toured the rural areas of the state he was both shocked and enlightened by what he saw. As he describes it: "And what interested me greatly was the poverty, misery, degradation of the people in certain sections . . . the lack of good food, the lack of ordinary comfort. . . . The first experience I had: I went into a little village called Monticello. Earl and Christenbery were with us, and there was an old man in his house, and on the mantel there were some old relics, a picture of Long and *Every Man a King*. This old man thought that these relics were his gods. There is one of the first indications of the temper of the people. Long had given them hope, had given them free ambulances, free hospitals, hot lunches, and things of that sort and the benefits. And they figured that Long was the one man for the first time in their

lives that was thinking about them. . . . When I saw
those old people—that is the thing I have never seen any
writer get on to. The people that I met on those trips—
poor. I never saw such poverty, the women with teeth so
full of tartar that they looked like coral shells. They
would come to those meetings at night in the cold and the
wet with babies wrapped up in blankets and use a flash-
light to find their way through the woods. They called
them speakings."

Another lawyer tried to put over much the same
thought to A. J. Liebling, finally resorting to a sports
figure of speech to clinch his point. The significance of
Longism, its great end result, he said, was that opportuni-
ties in the state had been opened up to people of all
classes: "Huey was like the kid who comes along in a
game of Chicago pool when all the balls are massed. He
breaks them and runs a few and leaves the table full of
shots for the other players. As long as the Longs are in,
you have a chance."

Many things have been said about Huey Long, mostly
bad, and while some of the criticisms have been unin-
formed others have been eminently right. But even after
the debits are written down in blackest ink one credit
stands out with peculiar significance for the record of
history. He forcibly introduced a large element of realism
into Southern politics. He asked the South to turn its
gaze from outside devils and the imagined past and take
a long, hard look at itself and the present. We have plenty
of problems, he said, but we can find the strength and the
resources to solve them ourselves. Gerald Johnson, who
heartily disliked him, could still say that Long was the
first Southerner since Calhoun to make an original contribution to the science of government. "I cherish profound
suspicion of his integrity, public and private," Johnson
wrote. "I regard his methods as detestable. Nevertheless,

the late Huey Pierce Long has the distinction of having
injected more realism into Southern politics than any
other man of his generation. Huey made millions of
Southerners think of the political problems of 1935 as
something quite different from those of 1865."

In Huey Long's vast plans there was no room for the
race issue. Racism was a false issue that would deflect
and divide people from the pursuit of the important objectives of politics; that would, in the revealing phrase
of Long leaders, "mess up his show." He never seriously
employed the race question in any of his campaigns,
either to win an election or to distract attention from
any failures in his own record. Apparently he had no
personal sense of race prejudice, and he seems to have
genuinely liked Negroes. By his own standards he was a
segregationist, but segregation entered into his thinking
only when it had to be related to politics. That is, he
did not consider it as an end in itself but as something that
might threaten or aid his political ends. Thus from the
beginning he included the Negroes, the poorest people
in the state, in his welfare programs. He did this not
out of altruism or idealism but for realistic economic
reasons. As one Long leader explained it to the writer:
"You can't help poor white people without helping
Negroes. But that's all right." At the same time, for
realistic political reasons he made no move to give the
vote to the Negroes, not because he had strong feelings
one way or the other on the subject, but because the
attempt could have no political significance. He would
have encountered fierce resistance, and he did not need
the Negro vote. On one occasion he discussed the race
situation in Louisiana for a Northern interviewer. The
reporter asked how he would treat Negroes under his
plan. "Treat them just the same as anybody else," Long
replied; "give them an opportunity to make a living."

Would he let them vote? "I'm not going into that. I'd leave it up to the States to decide as they want to. But in Louisiana a Negro's just the same as anybody else; he ought to have a chance to work and to make a living, and to get an education."

What Long did give the Negroes was more than they were getting in other Southern states. Being the realistic operator that he was, he knew that his course might stir white objections. He adopted a strategy of voicing publicly the familiar white attitudes on race relations and from behind this cover giving the Negroes some of the things they wanted. Unlike the businessmen of Reconstruction and the Populists, he did not label what he was doing; he seemed to be a complete segregationist. Once he explained to a Negro leader how he had managed to get better medical care for colored people: "Why, down in Louisiana . . . the whites have decided niggahs have got to have public health care. Got to give 'em clinics and good hospitals. Got to keep 'em healthy. That's fair and it's good sense. I said to them: 'You wouldn't want a colored woman watching over your children if she had pyorrhea, would you?' They see the point."

Sometimes the technique had a double edge. When the new Charity Hospital was built in New Orleans, some Negro leaders complained to Long that there were no colored nurses, when at least half the patients were Negroes. Huey said he would get their nurses in, but they would not like his method. He visited the hospital and then called a press conference. He was shocked at what he had found, he announced—white women were waiting on colored men, and it had to be stopped. Negroes might object to his method, indeed, and also white liberals, but he achieved his purpose by the only way that he could.

Huey's brother and first political heir, Earl Long, who

would win the governorship three times, either owned
or copied Huey's skill in dealing with both races. In the
last campaign that he made before his death Earl assured
colored audiences that he would take care of the question of integrated schools for them. He said, in practically these words: "Now, don't worry. I'm not going to
let them make you send your kids to schools with white
kids, where they'll lord it over 'em. You're going to have
your own schools."

Since Huey Long's death in 1935 elections in Louisiana
have been fought out between the two Democratic factions of Longs and anti-Longs, although splinter factions
often appear in the first primary. Factional candidates
for governor run at the head of a full ticket of suitors for
lesser offices, a practice rarely employed in other Southern
states, and the two principal factions are so specifically
defined as to constitute the equivalent of regular parties.
While the personality of a candidate may have some
influence, campaigns revolve almost entirely around
the issues laid down by Huey Long—taxation of the
corporate interests, extension of social welfare, enlarge-
ment of the state's regulatory powers. Any candidate for
governor who tries to break out of the pattern is practically doomed from the start. Thus in the election of
1960 the out-and-out segregationist aspirant, running on
the sole issue of segregation, polled only seventeen per
cent of the popular vote. He failed, as Earl Long, one
of the shrewdest analysts in the business, predicted he
would, because this issue alone was not enough in a race
where every candidate supported the principle of segregation.

The later heirs of Huey Long have adopted his strategy
in dealing with the race question. Under Earl Long the
benefits of social welfare were more abundantly bestowed
on the Negroes, who responded by voting the Long

ticket. Earl Long, going a step beyond Huey, encouraged the registration of Negroes as voters, the colored vote coming eventually to compose thirteen per cent of the total. His motives, like Huey's, were mixed and are not easily separated. Obviously the fact that he received the Negro vote had something to do with his thinking, but beyond that he seemed to feel, although he could never exactly define his reasons, that qualified Negroes should vote as a right. But essentially he was trying to do in a more difficult period what Huey had done, to subordinate the race issue to problems he considered more important. Earl Long always contended he did more to preserve the basic fabric of segregation than all the segregationists —and that the way to do it was by turning the attention of both races to normal political issues. Long leaders in the parishes have assured the writer that they have succeeded in blunting Negro militancy by dealing the Negroes into the suffrage and the welfare rewards.

When Earl Long had his tragic and much publicized collapse, he was trying to get a bill through the legislature that would have made it difficult for the segregationist groups to purge Negro voters from the rolls. Presumably his action qualified him for a place in the liberal heaven, but his purpose was not mentioned in the Northern press. Here, ran the accounts, was another comic Southern politician playing the usual part of the clown, acting as a Southern demagogue was supposed to act. Whatever Earl Long should have been criticized for, he was subjected to ridicule beyond his meed. It was the same sort of ridicule heaped upon the Populists by Northern commentators who had no conception of the obstacles against which the Populists had to fight. It was the same kind of derision visited upon Huey Long by liberals who had no realization of the dilemmas of liberalism in the South. The South will doubtless continue to wrestle with all its ancient problems and will move toward some solution. It can expect many pressures from the majority section, but it should look for little understanding. As Huey Long had known, it must find the answer in its own inner strength.